*The Mystery Religion
of W.B. Yeats*

The Mystery Religion of W.B. Yeats

Graham Hough

Emeritus Professor of English
University of Cambridge

THE HARVESTER PRESS   SUSSEX

BARNES & NOBLE BOOKS   NEW JERSEY

First published in Great Britain in 1984 by
THE HARVESTER PRESS LIMITED
Publisher: John Spiers
16 Ship Street, Brighton, Sussex

and in the USA by
BARNES & NOBLE BOOKS
81 Adams Drive, Totowa, New Jersey 07512

© Graham Hough, 1984

British Library Cataloguing in Publication Data
Hough, Graham
    The mystery religion of W.B. Yeats.
    1. Yeats, W.B—Knowledge—Occult
    sciences
    I. Title
    821'.8   PR5908.025
    ISBN 0-7108-0603-5

Library of Congress Cataloging in Publication Data
Hough, Graham Goulden, 1908–
    The mystery religion of W.B. Yeats.
    1. Yeats, W.B. (William Butler), 1865–1939—Knowledge
    —Occult sciences. 2. Yeats, W.B. (William Butler),
    1865–1939. A vision. 3. Occult sciences in literature.
    4. Poets, Irish—20th century—Biography. I. Title.
    PR5908.025H68   1984   821'.8   83-27560
    ISBN 0-389-20464-1

Typeset in 12 point Times by
Photobooks (Bristol) Ltd.
Printed in Great Britain by
Butler & Tanner Ltd, Frome and London

Εἰπεῖν· γῆς παῖς εἰμὶ καὶ οὐρανου ἀστερόεντος
αὐτὰρ ἐμοι γένος οὐράνιον·

Orphic Tablet

Contents

Preface

The first three chapters of this book were the Lord Northcliffe Lectures in Literature given at University College London in February 1983. I had set myself the rather difficult task of speaking about Yeats's occult philosophy not to professed Yeatsians but to a general literary audience. This meant a radical simplification, which I was anyway glad to attempt; for it has long seemed to me that Yeats studies were becoming so intricate and specialised that many of the readers he would have hoped for have abandoned the effort to follow his thought or see it in its context. I was only too conscious of how much I had had to leave out, particularly in reference to *A Vision*; so I have added a fourth chapter of rather a different kind, taking up some of the crucial difficulties of Yeats's final statement, in both its versions, with much closer reference to the text.

G.H.
May 1983

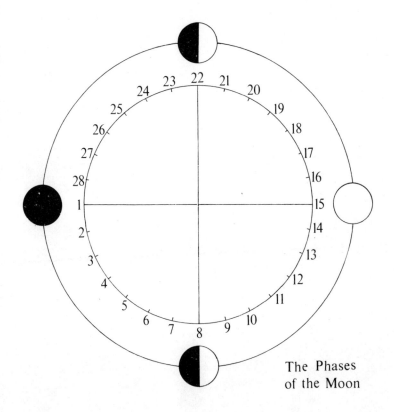

The Phases
of the Moon

I. The Occult Tradition

Just over fifty years ago Denis Saurat, at that time
Professor of French at London University, brought out
a book called *Literature and Occult Tradition*. Its sub-
title was *Studies in Philosophical Poetry*. To both these
concepts, occult tradition and philosophical poetry,
Saurat gave special meanings of his own. By occult
tradition he meant a vein of uninstitutional, speculative,
non-Christian religious activity, which makes inter-
mittent appearances in our culture from the Renaissance
on, which has a certain continuity or at least a tendency
to recur, and a certain degree of independence. By
philosophical poetry he meant to indicate a distinctively
post-Renaissance poetry with a basis in speculative
metaphysics that works to express 'the mind of modern
man'. The philosophical poet 'obtains a vision of the
far-off goals, expresses anew for his own time the
desires of his fellow men, marks out the distance
already covered or tries to divine the future ways. Thus
Milton in the 17th century, Goethe in the 18th, Victor
Hugo, Nietzsche and Whitman in the 19th'. And these

1

two elements turn out to be related; the philosophical poets use a body of common ideas that have their roots in what Saurat calls the occult tradition.

Literature and Occult Tradition was very much a pioneering work; it sketches the outline of a theory, and it gives a first example of 'philosophical' poetry in a discussion of the work of Spenser. Saurat's other books *Milton, Man and Thinker, Blake and Modern Thought* and *La Religion de Victor Hugo* contain detailed studies which were to support the theory. Much of this is pioneering work too, and some would say eccentric. Saurat takes as his examples of a heterodox, non-Christian imaginative tradition two poets who have generally been celebrated as outstanding champions of Christendom—Spenser and Milton. But Saurat sees their Christianity as a formal insertion into an edifice of a fundamentally different kind—like the Gothic shrine built inside the great mosque at Cordoba. And most readers have required more persuasion than Saurat is able to provide to convince them of that thesis. In the case of Milton, and to some extent Spenser too, he finds a main contributory stream to this current of ideas in the Cabala—that vast system of Jewish theosophy, existing primarily in and for the Hebrew world, which nevertheless made remarkable incursions into Western European thought during the Renaissance. Saurat has a good deal to say about the Cabala in *Literature and Occult Tradition*, but it would hardly have been possible for him to attempt a systematic account of this huge heterogeneous body of ideas, and indeed he does not attempt it. He would surely have been the first to admit that he has done no more than draw up a few more or less relevant bucketfuls from this shoreless ocean. So I don't think it can be said that Saurat's work was wholly successful or achieved what he intended. It was nevertheless important, for at a time when in literary circles at any rate a rather conventional kind of Geistesgeschichte was little questioned, it called attention to much that passed unnoticed—to the continual beating against the walls of received opinion by great waves of unorthodox and eccentric speculation. And I will not I hope be thought wanting in piety to my own masters if I say that the line of enquiry that Saurat sketched out was at least an interesting supplement to the Elizabethan world-picture and the seventeenth-century background.

Since Saurat's day even students of English literature —notoriously apt to slumber in out of date opinions— have been less inclined to accept those worn stereotypes: the medieval centuries as the Age of Faith, the Renaissance as a sudden efflorescence of secular enlightenment. Norman Cohn has made us aware of the millennial and eschatological movements of the late Middle Ages; C.S. Lewis reminded us that the heyday of spirit-lore was not some way back in the dark ages, but in the sixteenth century. Edgar Wind in *Pagan Mysteries* has drawn the outlines of the Orphic and Hermetic revival of the Renaissance, and D.P. Walker those of Spiritual and Daemonic Magic. Frances Yates has elucidated the Hermetic art and traced the early fortunes of the Rosicrucians; and the mysteries of the Cabala, never I suppose properly accessible except to Hebrew scholars, have now been given a lucid and accessible exposition in Gershom Scholem's great book *Main Trends in Jewish Mysticism*.[1] Much that once seemed merely eccentric now seems much less so. Blake, who even as late as T.S. Eliot's time could be thought of as the inventor of a fantastic private mythology, is now more easily connected with the established unorthodoxies of the past. So we are now a good deal less likely than we were forty or fifty years ago to think of our forebears as sitting comfortably in the middle of a respectable world-view with only a few anomalous intruders on the fringe. We can see without difficulty that much of the most spirited imaginative vision of every age was conveyed by massive movements far divergent from the ways of orthodoxy. And to establish this was a large part of Saurat's intention.

With this we can say farewell to Saurat—except for the title of his book, *Literature and Occult Tradition*. Saurat so far as I know is the first literary critic to talk of an occult tradition, thus bringing into consciousness an entity that the literary world had never formerly recognised; and my main purpose here is to call this idea in question. Is there such a thing as an occult tradition, in modern literature, and if so how are we to regard it? As a half-unconscious current of feeling, as an organised religious opposition, as a deplorable intellectual limbo, or as a serious movement of thought? The answers to these questions are not simple, and they are made no easier by the fact that the adherents of occult tradition, and their fellow-travellers, are apt to shroud it in a protective secrecy; while its detractors set upon it with considerable acrimony, often quite ill-informed. The idea of tradition itself is a highly debateable one. At the time Saurat was writing

4

the word tradition was under a good deal of pressure because of its use by Eliot in a famous essay. Eliot's influence at that time was very strong (I remember an American academic parody of that period called 'The Blessed Thomas Eliot Considered as the Air We Breathe'), and its whole tendency was to suggest, with a good deal of coercive persuasiveness, that for Western civilisation tradition (always used in the singular, as if there were only one) could only mean the tradition of Catholic Christian theological orthodoxy. There were of course plenty of people around who didn't want to hear about tradition at all, who were eager on the contrary to hail the appearance of various brave new worlds; but to those for whom the idea of tradition had any appeal it became almost axiomatic that it implied a high degree of philosophical and theological conformity. That there were other traditions of some imaginative validity was hardly allowed, and this had some curious effects on prevailing patterns of literary history. Eliot had some intermittent difficulty in fitting Shakespeare into his scheme of things—with the 'mixed and muddled scepticism of the Renaissance' as the best he could manage in the way of a philosophy. And the considerable tradition of Wordsworthian natural religion was pushed aside as though it were a minor English peculiarity, like herbaceous borders.

As far as modern literature was concerned the most strangely distorting effect was on the reputation of Yeats. It was evident from about 1930 that his was the most massive, powerful and intricate poetic talent of the age, and that this talent rested on a foundation of belief sufficiently consistent and coherent to be called a system. Yet this system of belief was unrecognised, unformulated, and largely opaque to the great majority of Yeats's readers. In all his writing Yeats insisted on the antique provenance of his faith, on his adherence to an age-old, world-wide creed: yet the great majority of his readers brushed all this aside as a negligible oddity or a regrettable aberration. The most extreme example is offered by Auden, who wrote in 1948 'How on earth, we wonder, could a man of Yeats's gifts take such nonsense seriously? . . . How *could* Yeats, with his great aesthetic appreciation of aristocracy, ancestral houses, ceremonial tradition, take up something so essentially lower-middle-class—or should I say Southern Californian—. . . Mediums, spells, the Mysterious Orient—*how* embarrassing.'² Views of this kind were widely held, though often less pungently expressed. It was supposed that Yeats somehow contrived to make great poetry out of ideas that were arbitrary, fantastic or merely absurd. This always seemed to me a grotesque contradiction; and I am glad to discover, on looking back, that writing in the same year as Auden I said then what I would still say; 'I do not think this is true, or even possible: the beliefs underlying any great poetry must represent a permanently or recurrently important phase of the human spirit, and cannot be merely individual or fashionable fantasy.' If ever the hypothesis of a rival tradition to the Eliotic one was needed, it was surely here, in the appreciation and understanding of Yeats's life and work. Indeed I believe it was the need to accommodate Yeats that played the largest part in bringing the idea of an occult tradition into the literary consciousness.

The Occult Tradition

This began to happen in the 1950s. I struck a few preliminary chords in my own book *The Last Romantics* in 1949, but the real beginning was Virginia Moore's book *The Unicorn* which came out in 1955—the first systematic attempt to expound Yeats's involvement with Hermetic, Rosicrucian and Cabalistic lore. The first, and in some ways still the best. It gives a fuller inventory of the sources of Yeats's speculative thought than any other single work. And it was done from scratch, when none of the currently available aids had come into existence. As she says with modest pride 'When I came to walk there it was virgin territory.' My reservations about Miss Moore's book are three. First that it is such a complete inventory that it is almost as confusing as the original documents; second, that in reaction to the Auden attitude it is almost indiscriminately willing to defend Yeats's ideas; and third, that it persistently tries to edge Yeats into the Christian fold, where I do not think he belongs.

Virginia Moore's work was followed by F.A.C. Wilson's *W.B. Yeats and Tradition* in 1958 and *Yeats's Iconography* in 1960. It will be noticed that here tradition again appears in the singular, as if there were only one. But this time tradition is not the Christian theological tradition, authorised by councils and blessed by the practice of the Church; it is a rival concern, but one which very soon, by usurping the singular title, begins to make a similar claim to authority and centrality. In some of the writing about the Blake/Yeats area at this time the occult tradition is referred to as 'the perennial philosophy', which in my young days used to mean something very different—St Thomas Aquinas.

7

And Wilson's second book *Yeats's Iconography* goes far to suggest that there is an officially sanctioned set of symbols in which 'the tradition' is expressed, and that anything outside this is mere decorative imagery. And so the occult tradition, having started as an anti-establishment tendency, begins to set itself up as a rival establishment, with anathemas, excommunications and short ways with dissenters.

I cannot say that I am very happy about this way of thinking, for all the learned foraging that has gone to support it. Having escaped from the somewhat assuming tones of Eliot's theologico-literary pronouncements, we seem to be running into another code with equally authoritarian pretensions and a similar restrictive effect on the free exercise of the imagination. So, though I do not by any means reject the idea of an occult tradition, I want to regard it with a somewhat wary eye. Tradition means something handed down, and it tends to suggest a lineal descent. From there it is an easy step to postulate a kind of orthodoxy, and that any diversion from the straight and narrow way is an impurity. And from here there begins to grow a strain of sectarian self-righteousness that is as alien to Yeats as it is to the spirit of poetry—and alien too to anything that is fertile and life-giving in the religio-philosophical ideas we are considering. Yeats's heritage of beliefs, themes, myths and symbols is too various to be compressed within such limits, and it is hard to find a single uniting thread or a single essential idea at the root of it. In Yeatsian criticism it is generally considered bad form to acknowledge a debt to modern philosophy; but one thing we have all learnt from modern philosophy is that the search for essence, for a single common factor in diverse but related phenomena, is often a mistake. We have learnt from Wittgenstein that if we *look and see* we shall not find in such a grouping something that is common to all, but similarities, relationships, and a whole series of them at that. These are what Wittgenstein, in several well-known passages, calls 'family resemblances'—'for the various resemblances between the members of a family: build, features, colour of eyes, gait, temperament, etc., overlap and criss-cross in the same way.' That is the sense in which we can speak of an occult tradition. The various doctrines, sects, philosophical schools that may be held to make up such a tradition do not constitute an orthodoxy, have not a single factor common to all, but they are related to each other in this sort of way. And if we understand that the relationships are of this kind, we shall be able to see that they are numerous and of long standing—much longer than Saurat in the early days of this enquiry was apt to suspect.

Donald Davie in the introduction to his *Oxford Book of Christian Verse* describes Yeats as a member of a non-Christian Church whose doctrine has yet to be formulated. In a rigorous sense this is true, but I think we can get nearer to a formulation than this would suggest; and that is what I now want to do—to give a broad outline of the main tenets of the occultist complex and some indication of where they are to be found, so that we shall know where to situate Yeats on the intellectual map. At first sight this may seem unnecessary, as by now there are so many works offering to do something of this kind. Some of these are studies of Yeats, some are histories of modern occultism, some are devotional and theological works of the occultist creed. I am deeply in debt to their assiduity and learning, but I am also, I must confess, less than satisfied. If at the end of it all Donald Davie can find that the Yeatsian creed has not yet been formulated, then these works of exposition have not done their work with complete success. In some cases at least, the assiduity and learning have become so elaborate that they have become an obstacle; they have made Yeats not more accessible but less. My effort therefore will be towards a radical simplification. We are not venturing into an untrodden wilderness, but rather into a garden of forking paths. I shall endeavour to choose those that lead most directly to the centre.

The first difficulty we encounter is that of recognising the presence of a powerful religious impulse in a setting from which the dispositions and feelings that we habitually associate with religion are lacking. A.P. Sinnett, the theosophical writer who gave Yeats his earliest introduction to occultist thinking, is quite frank about this. 'Spirituality, in the occult sense' he writes, 'has nothing to do with feeling devout: it has to do with the capacity of the mind for assimilating knowledge at the fountainhead of knowledge itself.' The result of this attitude is that the mainspring of occultist activity seems nearer to curiosity than to devotion. The element of personal devotion is indeed often absent, for at the summit of the occultist cosmogony there is no personal God. Anthropomorphic language inevitably finds its way in, but it is as a language of accommodation. The ultimate reality is one to which no phenomenal attributes or qualifications can be applied. We find neither the Jehovah of the Old Testament who speaks out of the whirlwind, nor the loving father of Christianity. Instead we have an 'Omnipresent, Eternal, Boundless, and Immutable Principle on which all speculation is impossible.' This Principle is so utterly transcendent that 'it cannot properly either be named, or spoken of, or conceived by opinion, or be known, or perceived by any being.' No qualities can be attributed to it, for any attribution is a limitation, and it is limitless. Since its nature is generative of all things, it is not any one of them. 'Neither, therefore, is it a certain thing, nor a quality, nor a quantity, nor intellect, nor soul, nor that which is moved, nor again that which stands still. Nor is it in place, or in time; but is by itself uniform, or rather without form, being prior to all form, to motion and to permanency.' The formulation I have just quoted is a pastiche from Theosophy and Neoplatonism; but of course the same could be found in a multitude of sources. It is the One of Plotinus, the Brahman of Indian religious philosophy, the *to apeiron*, the Boundless, of the Pre-Socratics, the Ain Soph of the Cabala. The connection of such an Absolute with the multitudinous variety of the world must always be obscure. It has been said that 'The abstract idea of absolute fullness has no determination to distinguish it from the abstract idea of absolute emptiness'; and in its austere archetypal form a religion of this kind has dispensed with all the allurements of feeling and imagery that attend more popular faiths. But as we shall see it does not often remain in that pristine condition.

11

Religion implies not only a conception of God, but of the soul's relation to God. What is the status of the human soul in a faith of this type? Inconsistently perhaps, or by any one of numerous theological strategies, the individual soul is perceived as of the same substance as the divine Absolute—either as a spark from the boundless light, or as really identical with it, separated only by illusion—the possibilities are endless. At all events as we know it the soul is divided from its true nature, or has fallen into generation or material life—again the formulations are many; and its proper destiny is to return whence it came and to achieve again its real being. This may mean a total identification with the Absolute, a kind of annihilation, or the continuation of individual existence in some heavenly world—to be achieved after death, or more usually, after many lives and many deaths; or temporarily in moments of ecstasy in this life.

The aim is union with or assimilation to the God; and the relation is not that of the child to the father or of creature to creator. The infinite and unbounded One clearly cannot be a creator-God, maker of heaven and earth, in the manner of the first chapter of Genesis, of the Nicene creed, and of popular Christianity ever since. Accordingly we find in occultist thought that the idea of creation falls into the background, and is replaced by a doctrine of emanation, in one form or another; or of continual emanations. 'We believe in no *creation*', writes Madame Blavatsky 'but in the periodical and consecutive appearance of the universe from the subjective on to the objective plane of being, at regular intervals of time . . .'[3] These emanations occur 'without thinking, without perception, without intention, without resolve, without emotion, without desire'; and they leave the unknown Godhead unmodified and unchanged.

There are endless philosophical difficulties in conceiving such a process. How can the absolute, the undetermined, submit to determination? How can the unmanifest manifest itself without abnegating its own nature? A great variety of images can be found, all more or less inadequate, to symbolise what cannot be described in terms of sense. In the Cabala the boundless, the unmanifest, reveals itself as boundless light; the light concentrates itself into a point, and the point of light becomes the first manifestation of the deity in the lower world. Or, in a later Cabalistic formula, the Absolute by an act of self-limitation withdraws from a certain part of its own being, and this forms the first sphere of the manifest world. This first manifestation can be seen as a demiurge, a subsidiary deity who is the creator of the world, as among the Gnostics and the Neoplatonists. A further manifestation is the Anima Mundi, the Soul of the World, a divine principle pervading the universe with all its imperfections, yet without compromising the impassibility and perfection of the One. Most generally this way of thinking takes the form of a series of emanations, each giving rise to the next, and becoming successively more limited, more bounded by form and image, more concrete, till in the end we arrive at the material world, the world of sense in which we live. This is the scheme of the Cabala, with its ten Sephiroth or spheres of being. Various barriers, gulfs, abysses, falls are conceived to occur

13

between the higher and the lower levels of such a scale, and sometimes the higher and the lower are simply set against each other; but the lower is always seen as an echo of the higher. Hence the oft repeated Hermetic maxim *Quod superius sicut quod inferius*—As above so below.

This kind of cosmology—a world of successive emanations, each a degree further from the One—can take many forms, and perhaps more important, these can result in very different scales of value. To some of the Gnostic sects of the early centuries of the Christian era the demiurge, the secondary deity who creates the world, was evil; the material world was evil, and the only business of the devotee was to escape from it. But in other forms of Gnosticism, and notably in the Cabala God is equally present in all the emanations,[4] is in Malkuth, the sphere of matter, as much as in Kether, the point of pure uncontaminated light. Indeed in one symbolisation the higher part of the realm of being is called the King, and Malkuth the lowest is called his Bride. In the Neoplatonism of Plotinus, if I understand it rightly, there is a good deal of ambiguity. Plotinus, we are told, lived 'as if he were ashamed to be in the body'; and the right course of life was the familiar Platonic ladder, rising from the material to the intellectual world, and destroying the rungs beneath you as you go. But he refused to say that matter was evil; in fact he talks about 'the grandeur and beauty of the world of sense', even though it is the final duty of the philosophic aspirant to abandon it for the world of ideas. And many of the fellow-travellers who sailed under the flag of Neoplatonism were obviously far more entangled with the phenomenal world.

14

As might be expected, these various cosmological views give rise to various ethical valuations. Those to whom matter is evil, those to whom it is neutral, and those to whom it is a part of the divine substance are likely to develop very different views of man's life in the flesh and the duties entailed by it. Even a single cosmology may result in two diametrically opposite moral codes. Among the Gnostics who believed that life in the body was worthless and evil there were some who deduced from this the duty of asceticism and celibacy, and others who thought that a life of total sensual abandonment was perfectly in order, since none of these earthly matters were of any importance. This kind of ambiguity is apt to persist even within the breast of the individual professor of the occultist creed. Every reader of Blake must have been puzzled by the extraordinary contradictions in his view of the natural world and the natural life. And in Yeats there is the notorious opposition between the ethereal love poetry of his early days and the work of the fierce old man who said he could be stirred only by lust and rage.

The emanationist view of the phenomenal universe has another consequence. Instead of a sharp opposition between God and the world it presents a graded hierarchy of being, and so allows for a number of intermediate powers, between the One and the world we live in. The first of these is *psyche tou Kosmou*, the *Anima Mundi*, the Soul of the World, a conception with a long life and great powers of revival under new names. It goes back to Plotinus, and even to Plato himself; and it reappears in this century as the Astral Light of the Theosophists and the Collective Unconscious

15

of Jungian psychology. It is possible to give this World-Soul a philosophical interpretation, or even a foundation in empirical psychology, as Jung said he did; but when we descend lower in the scale of being, to the ranks of subordinate gods and daimons we begin to enter the realm of almost unbridled fantasy. In late antiquity the stars were gods, and in popular Neoplatonism there was a host of sidereal deities. Chief among these are the planetary gods, who because of the immense and universal influence of astrology survived as substantial powers throughout the Christian era, and still do to our own day, as you can see by consulting the appropriate column in the evening paper. The elaborate classification of the choirs of angels which scholastic theology inherited from the pseudo-Dionysius is a Christianisation of the same tradition, and at times when syncretist tendencies were dominant the ancient gods and heroes with their pagan names were easily identified in one way or another with the angels and demons of Christian mythology. There was thus a continual penetration of occultist beliefs into the fringe regions of orthodoxy. The advantages of such beliefs for poetry can hardly be exaggerated. We have only to recall what they did for Milton. The fallen angel who designed Pandemonium, Satan's palace in hell, is identified with Hephaestus, Vulcan or Mulciber, the craftsman of the Olympian gods.

Nor was his name unheard or unadored
In ancient Greece; and in Ausonian land
Men called him Mulciber; and how he fell
From Heaven they fabled, thrown by angry Jove

Sheer o'er the crystal battlements: from Morn
To Noon he fell, from Noon to dewy Eve,
A Summer's day; and with the setting Sun
Dropt from the Zenith like a falling Star,
On Lemnos th'Aegean Isle: thus they relate,
Erring.

The host of daimons who fill up the intermediate
spaces between heaven and earth are identified in
various ways. Besides the planetary gods astrology
furnished a profusion of lesser powers—the decans, for
example, or rulers of each ten degrees of the zodiacal
circuit. In the system of Paracelsus we have the spirits
of the elements, earth, air, fire and water—gnomes
sylphs, salamanders and undines. And these of course
are the fairies of popular tradition, still connected with
the elements in Shakespeare (it was the quarrels of
Oberon and Titania that caused the bad weather of the
summer of 1594) but identified by later folklorists
rather with the spirits of the dead. Once we postulate
the presence of these intermediate powers we open up
the possibility of communicating with them, of gaining
their help and friendship, or even of commanding
them—Demonic Magic, in fact; Faustus and Prospero
and Cornelius Agrippa. It is this that accounts for
much of the moral ambiguity of occultist belief and
practice. The ultimate goal of all commerce with spirits
must be the supreme Spirit, union with the One, and for
those whose aspiration is wholly to this union, habit
and imagination are so austerely disciplined as to leave
little or no communication with the world of human
passions and activities. But many, perhaps most,

17

occultists do not aim so high; their ambition is to communicate with spirits of lower rank, for purposes nearer to ordinary mundane desires, power or love or riches. And these endeavours may be benign, as those of Prospero were, or they may descend to the repulsive imaginings of the *Malleus Maleficarum*.

We can view all this of course with amiable tolerance as a branch of spiritual archaeology. But there comes a time, in reading Plutarch or Apuleius or D.P. Walker or Frances Yates, when one feels impelled to ask, What is the real status of these beliefs? How seriously were they held? Were they ever seriously held at all? And to this I think we cannot give any firm answer. We can say, as a number of scholars have, that *mystères littéraires*, mere poetic metaphors, are often mistaken for *mystères cultuels*, objects of cult and devotion.[5] But I doubt whether the line between them can be so sharply drawn.

What is most notable in this realm of intermediate powers is the smooth transition between serious philosophical cosmology and merely fanciful indulgence. The idea of subordinate daimonic powers begins with the need to explain how it can be that the limitless, inconceivable, indescribable Absolute can submit itself to contingency. It ends in a riot of fancy with hardly more serious purpose than a nursery tale. And the poets love to linger in this middle region, where the image-making faculty is free to invent, adapt or borrow as it likes, but can still retain a connection with metaphysical truth. So Milton is able to take a holiday from hell and enjoy a short parachute drop with one of the Olympian gods; and his conscience is clear in doing

18

so because the whole story is only a distorted version of something that really happened—the fall of the rebel angels.

Few things in this world-view are immediately obvious, and it lends itself to endless elaboration. To approach it *knowledge* is required. It is not demanded of followers of the occult tradition that they become as little children. On the contrary, salvation is attained by acquiring a difficult and hidden gnosis. For this reason all adherents of this complex of beliefs are sometimes described as Gnostics; in that sense rightly, though this should not be taken to imply an identification in other respects with the Gnostic sects of the early Christian centuries. Salvation by knowledge, then, as opposed to salvation by faith or good works. In contrast with the ethical intensity and the ethical absolutism of Christianity, it is very noticeable that beyond a requirement of ritual purity there is generally no very distinct moral orientation in the occultist schemes of salvation, and no appeal to mankind as a whole. The knowledge that leads to union with the One is typically hidden knowledge, only to be acquired by initiation into a closed group. This runs right through the centuries, from the ancient mysteries to the various occult fellowships of our own day, and in many cases a vow of secrecy is exacted, with heavy spiritual penalties for those who reveal hidden matters. Hence the phenomenon that seems to occur in all ages and in every political condition—the more or less secret society of believers that selects its own members and puts them through a special course of training.

Here we reach a region where the arbitrary and the

fantastic begin to have free rein. We start with a rational speculative exploration, in tune with the most responsible philosophical thought of its day; we end with a riotous profusion of prescriptions, magic formulas, rituals and symbolic texts, incubated in the carefully protected hothouses of hidden cults. Some of these symbolic elements are widespread and recurrent —a Jungian would say archetypal, permanent and universal configurations of the human mind. For example, certain numbers, the trinity and the quaternity; certain massive features of the physical world, the sun the moon and the planets; certain human relationships, parent and child, marriage. We can think of these as forming as it were a repository of natural symbolism, which religion could hardly avoid making use of. But some are entirely arbitrary, accidental and local. They have simply been made up, by individual practitioners —Paracelsus, Madame Blavatsky, Aleister Crowley; they can be traced to chance images or irresponsible inventions. But they have found their way into the symbolic language of a sect and so acquired a spurious authority. After a few years they are solemnly incorporated into the deposit of inherited wisdom. And it is this element of the arbitrary and fantastic grotesquely investing itself with supposed authority that accounts for a large part of the contempt and dislike which occult movements attract to themselves.

Where does the authority, the supposed authority come from? In almost all cases the answer is the same. It is ancient wisdom, handed down from some sage, demigod or deity in the remote past; or it is the lore of an antique race. The Hermetic philosophy is derived from Hermes Trismegistus, who was identified with the Egyptian god Thoth, who was identified with the Greek Hermes, but was also thought to be a human magus, an elder contemporary of Moses. In the Cambridge University Library, I am happy to say, the Hermetic writings are still catalogued under his name. Orpheus plays the same role in the Orphic mysteries. The doctrines of the Rosicrucians, whatever they are, for it is not easy to find out, are the sum of the wisdom gathered in the near east by Father Christian Rosenkreuz, who lived, according to the documents on which the Brotherhood is founded, at the end of the fourteenth century. The races most favoured as repositories of ancient wisdom were the Chaldeans, the Egyptians and latterly, as those who follow the current development of these matters will know, the inhabitants of Atlantis. And even when the claims to antiquity are less extreme it is nearly always the case that the current exponent of an occult doctrine professes to have received it from some older predecessor. The rituals of the Golden Dawn, the society to which Yeats belonged, were founded on 'an old Rosicrucian manuscript', written in cypher, whose provenance is variously described, but according to one account was from a bookstall in Farringdon Street. Teachings are frequently ascribed to occult masters, living or dead, and are said to have been handed on secretly by oral tradition—a claim which it is equally difficult either to substantiate or to refute. The doctrines of the Cabala were given by the Lord to Abraham; or to Moses at the same time as the Tables of the Law, but they were unwritten and were transmitted only to initiates. And the chain of oral

21

tradition goes on to quite modern times. Madame Blavatsky of the Theosophical Society and McGregor Mathers of the Golden Dawn both had hidden instructors whom nobody else ever met, and Yeats had spirit guides who worked through the automatic writing of his wife.

Lastly, since the goal of all mystical and magical sects is ultimately deliverance, salvation, liberation from the manifold bonds and obstructions of earthly life, there is a profusion of beliefs about the life after death. As always with speculations about human survival, this teaching exists on every level, from the mundane fancies of a sort of endless picnic in the Elysian fields to an imageless contemplation of the Absolute from which all trace of human experience has disappeared. What is noticeable in the tradition we are considering is that the idea of reincarnation, in one form or another, has a strong tendency to recur. It is not universal, it is not of course part of orthodox Christian belief, and in the West it hardly attains the status of a formulated philosophical doctrine, as it does in the religions of the East. But from the Pythagoreans on it is always reappearing—among the Cathars of the Middle Ages, in the later Cabala, in a number of isolated poetic manifestations, and in profusion among modern sectaries, who are often as familiar with their previous incarnations as they are with their zodiacal signs. From the time of the Theosophical Society at the end of the last century, overtly founded on oriental doctrine, the origin of these ideas is exotic, and they are usually couched in Indian terminology. But the earlier instances are numerous and are apparently independent of Hindu or Buddhist influence.

It is now perhaps time to ask where this vast family of doctrines and symbolic teachings come from. Have they a common source? Can we think of the occult tradition in all its variety as springing from a single root? Or if not that, as growing up in a unique seed-bed? Obviously the accounts of doctrinal origins we have glanced at were mythical—the objects of a tender respect or of mere ridicule, largely according to the terms in which the claims are couched, or the setting in which they occur. When the Cabalists say that they received their doctrine on Mount Sinai we can easily accept this as a symbolic way of saying that Cabalist teaching is an authentic part of holy wisdom. But the story of Father Christian Rosenkreuz hardly rises above the level of psychic romance. And when Madame Blavatsky talks of her mentors Morya and Koot Hoomi, to outsiders at least the odour of humbug becomes uncomfortably strong. But behind all these mythical claims to ancient origin there lies, or can be thought to lie, the quite truthful assertion that much of this doctrine is very old, as old as the record of human speculation; some can be said to be almost indigenous to the human mind. And this leads to the idea of a common substratum of human imagination, the Jungian collective unconscious—to my mind a perfectly rational hypothesis with a good deal of empirical support. However, I take it when we ask where it all came from we are looking for an answer in more positive historical terms. And although my purpose is not historical I think we can at least sketch out such an answer.

The occultists' claims to a mythical antiquity begin

to congeal into a certain historicity in the Greek world of the sixth century B.C. Already at this time, outside the worship of the Olympian gods, the state cults, the conservative party at prayer, we find certain mystical sects, characterised by initiations, the search for union with the god, a belief in an afterlife of purgation and reward and a sense of separation from the rest of the world, marked by certain abstinences and rules of life. I am speaking of the Orphic sects and the Pythagoreans who were later identified or confused with them. With them we are still only on the fringe of history, and in territory that scholars still dispute. The mystery cults however persist all over the Greek world; one of them, the Eleusinian, even became part of the Athenian religious establishment. Orphic and Pythagorean sects continue through the classical period; echoes and references are found in the drama—in Euripides and Aristophanes. Above all, Plato, though contemptuous of the ritualist and superstitious side of Orphism is in the mystical and mythological part of his teaching deeply penetrated by Orphic and Pythagorean influence.

But these are exceptions and excretions to world-views and philosophies basically conceived in other terms. There was to come a time, five hundred years later, when the mystical and mythological side of Platonism, the magical and superstitious side of the mystery cults, were to revive, to fuse and melt into a new amalgam. And it is here, in the Graeco-Roman world of late antiquity, in the earliest Christian centuries, that we can first clearly recognise the features of what we have tentatively called the occult tradition. The authorities appealed to by later occultists, whatever their fabulous claims, in fact almost all belong to this world. It is in this ambience that Neoplatonism arose, and in Neoplatonism, ranging as it does from the severe and rational metaphysic of Plotinus to the rankest growth of credulity and superstition, we can find traces of all the doctrines we have mentioned. This is the time of the Gnostic sects, Christian and non-Christian, with their claims to secret wisdom. The writings attributed to Hermes Trismegistus actually date from the second and third centuries A.D., and the Cabala, though its first written records are medieval, appears to rest on traditions that go back to the same period. It was a time of religious syncretism, when the cult of the old gods had declined, had revived again with a changed emphasis, and had been added to, not to say swamped, by new cults and deities coming from the East—notably Persia and Egypt. The chapter on the third century in Dean Inge's study of Plotinus[6] offers a concise historical illustration of practically all the ideas and tendencies we have been considering. I will quote a few sentences from Inge's synopsis of this chapter.

He remarks on the decline of Greek and Roman racial stock and the growing influx of a cosmopolitan population. This, he says, 'profoundly affected the social life, the morals and religion of the Empire. . . . The revival of the religious sentiment was strongly marked. Toleration and fusion of cults were general. . . . The old gods were again honoured; but the religions of the East were far more potent.' And he goes on to describe the characteristics of the worship of Isis, Cybele and Attis, and Mithra. 'The new syncretism differed widely from the old polytheism. It was now the

25

fashion to worship one God with many names.' . . .
There was a great revival of superstition, especially of
magic, white and black, and of astrology, which was
called the queen of the sciences. . . . Eschatology is
always vague and contradictory, but it is clear that
belief in immortality was much stronger in the 3rd
century than in the first. . . . The Orphic and Pytha-
gorean faiths and the Oriental cults owe much of their
attractiveness to their definite promises of a future life.
The revival of the "mysteries" was not unconnected
with the same tendency.'

If I had more time and more temerity I would like to
enlarge on the kinship between the mystery religions of
the ancient world and the modern revival of occultism
in which Yeats is involved. One of the Orphic tablets on
the entry of the soul into the afterlife looks amazingly
like a first draft of a poem by Yeats—a sequel perhaps
to 'Sailing to Byzantium'. But from one who is not a
classical scholar such musings would be quite idle, and
would in any case leave us fifteen hundred years from
the *fin-de-siècle* which is our destination. We have
paused at the beginning of the Christian centuries, and
if we wanted to trace the survival of occultist tendencies
through the Middle Ages we would have to look to
magic of the Dr Faustus kind; to heretical sects such as
the Cathars; to sciences of doubtful status and repute—
astrology and alchemy. C.G. Jung has indeed made an
extensive study of alchemy that sees it as the bearer
through the centuries of a concealed spiritual philosophy.
Then at the Renaissance the ancient mysteries reappear
in full panoply. The Platonic philosophies, speculative
metaphysics and magical arts of the fifteenth and

26

sixteenth centuries are to a large extent simply a revival of the syncretism of late antiquity. Their practitioners are not mere mountebanks, but include great names— Ficino, Pico della Mirandola, Paracelsus and Cornelius Agrippa. It must I think seem to the modern student who surveys this corpus of writing that there is a continuous and uncriticised gradation from propositions that are substantially acceptable, through the evidently mythological, the merely metaphoric, the simply fictitious, to the flatly fraudulent. And it is likely that the modern student has no taste for trying to find a foothold on this slippery slope. But it does not alter the fact that many of the great and good have done so. Descartes was interested in the Rosicrucians, Newton in the mystical interpretation of Scripture; Goethe was an alchemist.

From the Renaissance on there are continual appearances of brotherhoods, sects, societies that carry on some part or other of the occultist programme. In the early seventeenth century the publication in Germany of certain documents about a mystic Brotherhood, called the Rosicrucians after their founder Father Christian Rosenkreuz, aroused great excitement. At first, to be sure, there were no actual Rosicrucians, only manifestoes, of a spiritual-alchemical cast. The awe-struck curiosity they evoked was all the greater because apart from a general air of mystery, their doctrine was not very clearly defined, so that the Rosicrucian canopy was able to shelter a variety of religious revolutionaries, caballists and aspiring magicians. In the eighteenth century a number of groups adopting the Rosicrucian name and purpose actually came into existence in

France and Germany, and added their weight to the numerous quasi-magical societies with which the age of reason was honeycombed. These were joined and abetted in the later eighteenth century by esoteric branches of freemasonry which themselves merged with the extensive French revival of occultism in the mid-nineteenth century. The leaders of this movement, Eliphas Levi, Stanislas de Guaita and Sar Peladan have been much discussed in recent years, and their impact on French Romantic and Symbolist literature is well known. From there it is only a step across the Channel to the Order with which Yeats is most closely associated—the Order of the Golden Dawn, essentially continuous with the continental movements, and linked to them in several ways.

This summary, absurdly condensed as it is, has a purpose. It is to call attention to a paradox. Almost every specific claim made by these modern occultist fraternities to ancient authority is dubious, or mistaken, or simply false. Yet the underlying claim to ancient lineage, to belong to a train of belief and practice that goes as far back as sober history can reach—that is true, and even demonstrably true. But these early outlines necessarily remain obscure. More definitely I tried to locate the cradle of the occult tradition in the Graeco-Roman world of late antiquity. This may seem an unpromising starting-point for the world-view of a poet whose active career lies between 1890 and 1939. But let us look back for a moment to this period, to the passage I have already quoted, to Dean Inge's account of the third century AD. It describes a world in which the old gods have lost their power, in which a wave of alien immigration in the human realm has been parallelled by a similar cosmopolitanism in the divine world. New doctrines from the East have appeared, with new claims—exclusive claims among the simpler-minded devotees, but among the sophisticated a wide-embracing acquiescence; all religions are one. The appeal is no longer to the gods of the city, the gods of Hellas or of Rome; it is to a new universalism, that professing to unite, paradoxically tends to divide. This is the century in which the occult tradition takes its rise. But as we contemplate this picture, surely we find that its features are not strange to us. Do we not recognise them, in a slightly altered guise? Could not this description be applied, with a few small modifications, to the century just passed—the century that extends from the early years of Yeats to our own day?

II. Yeats's Beliefs

In considering questions of belief we must not confuse
the formal statement of a creed, or the philosophical
unravelling of its implications, with the concrete
religious experience of the individual. A child brought
up in a traditionally religious household is not presented
with a theology, or a definite moral code. Habits,
injunctions, images, fragmentary ideas and precepts
are imprinted on his mind, and it is only gradually, if
at all, that he becomes aware that they are part of a
system. And for one like Yeats, who had to excavate his
own religious tradition from a mass of miscellaneous
debris, this is even more obviously true. He grew into
his occultism continuously; a true gnostic, in the
restricted sense of the term, he was continuously
increasing his knowledge; and to show in detail the
steps by which this occurred would be to write his
spiritual biography, a formidable task which has not
yet been fully attempted.

From early childhood Yeats was always acutely
sensitive to religious impressions; the peculiarity of his

religious upbringing was that it was largely self-contradictory. The family background was solid prosaically Protestant Church of Ireland, and it seems to have left no lasting impression on his mind, beyond a residual sense of guilt and a strong conviction that he was not a Catholic. And what might have been drawn from this source was largely cancelled by the influence of his father, that mercurial and protean character, who among other things was a nineteenth-century agnostic, with an avowed allegiance to Huxley, Tyndall and John Stuart Mill. This contradiction betwen habitual churchgoing and his father's unbelief was likely to arouse the boy's questioning instincts, and left him a space to evolve in his own way, as a monolithic orthodoxy would not.

Writing of himself as a young man he said:

> I am very religious, and deprived by Huxley and Tyndall, whom I detested, of the simple-minded religion of my childhood, I had made a new religion, almost an infallible church of poetic tradition, of a fardel of stories, and of personages, and of emotions, inseparable from their first expression, passed on from generation to generation by poets and painters, with some help from philosophers and theologians. I wished for a world where I could discover this tradition perpetually, and not in pictures and in poems only, but in tiles round the chimney-piece and in the hangings that kept out the draught. I had even created a dogma: "Because those imaginary people are created out of the deepest instinct of man, to be his measure

and his norm, whatever I can imagine those mouths speaking may be the nearest I can go to truth." When I listened they seemed always to speak of one thing only: they, their loves, every incident of their lives, were steeped in the supernatural.

(A 115)

In Sligo as an adolescent he had already been fascinated by the ghost stories and fairy tales of the countryside, and with a cousin had seen mysterious lights moving about the hills at night.

From that on I wandered about raths and fairy hills and questioned old women and old men and, when I was tired out or unhappy, began to long for some such end as True Thomas found. I did not believe with my intellect that you could be carried away body and soul, but I believed with my emotions, and the belief of the country people made that easy. . . . I began telling people that one should believe whatever had been believed in all countries and periods, and only reject any part of it after much evidence, instead of starting all over afresh and only believing what one could prove.

(A 78)

Already we can see the outline of a doctrine that was to be a permanent part of the furniture of Yeats's mind—the prestige of ancient wisdom, the authority of the folk-memory and its images.

Reveries over Childhood and Youth and *The Trembling*

of the Veil, from which these passages come, are works of haunting poetic beauty. Yeats is as much of an enchanter in prose as in verse, and the charm of such paragraphs as these has contrived to produce the misleading impression that Yeats's early beliefs were purely literary in their inspiration, derived from folk-tales and romantic poetry. Far too much has been made of Yeats as the self-indulgent collector of fairy-tales and Irish bric-à-brac. Auden, in the essay from which I have quoted, goes on to suggest that Yeats's beliefs were purely aesthetic, adopted not because they were true but because they were picturesque. This is quite wrong. From an early age Yeats was making systematic enquiry into spiritual matters; and if anyone is still inclined to believe that he was seduced by their aesthetic charm, I can only recommend the perusal of some of Yeats's actual sources—Madame Blavatsky's *Isis Unveiled*, A.P. Sinnett's *Esoteric Buddhism*, and Israel Regardie's volumes on the Golden Dawn, which from a literary point of view must stand high among the most repulsive works of the later nineteenth century. Yeats read them for their content. He could be caricatured as a dreamy stripling, and often was; but in fact he was also a great systematiser, always attracted by elaborate schematic creeds, whether well-founded or not. And in pursuit of what he felt to be obscured or neglected truth he was serenely willing to keep company from which the mere aesthete would have recoiled in dismay.

We can divide the main influences on Yeats's religious development into four phases—none of them literary, none of them having any connection with poetry and the arts. They succeed each other in a rough chronology, but partly overlap, with influences from one spreading into the others. They are: first, the Theosophical Society, under its leader Madame Blavatsky; second, the magical society known as the Order of the Golden Dawn; third, psychical research and spiritualism; and fourth, the synthesis Yeats eventually arrived at, set forth in the two versions of his book *A Vision*, 1925 and 1937.

To begin, then, at the beginning. A Dublin friend, Charles Johnston, had fallen under the influence of the Theosophists and in 1885, together with Yeats and a few others, founded the Dublin Hermetic Society, to discuss all the occult sciences and pseudo-sciences of the day—Odic force, Spiritualism, Esoteric Buddhism —which last was the name then often given to the Theosophic adaptation of Indian thought. The young Dublin hermetists were of course only one of innumerable groups about this time who were attracted to such explorations. We can aptly recall the words used by Dean Inge to describe the third century A.D.: the old gods were losing their power; exotic divinities from the East were coming to take their place; and the allurements of these eclectic theologies might lead in almost any direction, from the practice of magic to the quasi-scientific investigations of the Society for Psychical Research. The dominant influence on the group to which Yeats belonged was the Theosophical Society. This is by now a world-wide movement and has gone through many changes; at this time it was ten years old and still dominated by its founder, Madame Blavatsky, recently established in London when the Yeats family moved to London in 1887. Yeats immediately joined the London Lodge of the Theosophists, falling strongly under Madame's influence. So without any doubt it was Theosophy that gave Yeats his first systematic introduction to the occult tradition, and for those who want to take his beliefs seriously this solves certain problems but raises others. It solves many problems, for again and again we find that obscure, puzzling and apparently original elements in Yeats's esoteric doctrine, even towards the end of his life, turn out to have their roots in the Theosophical teaching he first encountered in his early twenties. And once we begin to look into it, this is not surprising.

Helena Petrovna Blavatsky was an extraordinary woman, one of several peripatetic Russian sages who established themselves as spiritual leaders around the turn of the century. Her career can be parallelled with those of Gurdjieff and Ouspensky, or that all-purpose Egeria, Lou-Andreas Salomé. In some way, no one quite knows how, she had accumulated an astonishing mass of occult mythology and theory. This is set forth in the vast farrago of her first book *Isis Unveiled* (1877), and its slightly more orderly successor *The Secret Doctrine* (1887). These purport to be a synthesis of all the great world religions, older than any of them, communicated to Madame by hidden Masters or Mahatmas who lived beyond the Himalayas. They are madly eclectic works, reckless in their mixture of Hindu and Buddhist material with a comprehensive selection of Western occultist lore—Hermetic, Neo-platonic, Cabalistic and Rosicrucian. To a traditionally cultivated mind they are singularly tasteless compilations. But embedded in them are the essentials of the occultist doctrine, quite accurately presented. Madame Blavatsky was a perfect magpie for picking up doctrine and symbolism from a bewildering multitude of sources. She had collaborators, and sometimes recruited assistance in expounding the ideas of certain historical periods. Some of her authorities were genuine, some were not. A good deal she just made up. But what she makes up is on the whole harmonious with what she derives from other sources, and when she cites an identifiable authority—a Neoplatonic philosopher, for example—it generally turns out that she gives a fair representation of what he actually said. And either she or one of her assistants had considerable powers of synthesis. After I had written the first chapter, in which I tried to present a sort of Identikit picture of occult doctrine through the ages, I thought I would look up Madame Blavatsky's *Outline of Theosophy* (1891), a short handbook in which she gives a summarised introduction to Theosophical teaching, shorn of the profuse mythological trappings. And I discovered to my surprise that practically everything I had written was to be found there, in a very lucid and comprehensible form. So again contrary to the general literary belief, if Yeats was introduced to the occultist creed via the Theosophical Society it was probably the best introduction he could have found, and one which gave him copious references to the more ancient parts of the tradition.

But now for the awkward problems. Madame Blavatsky must be given due credit for her huge fund of out-of-the-way learning, her organising power and her immense personal magnetism. But it must also be said that she was a mystery-monger, a charlatan and a cheat, of a sordidly commonplace kind. Her career as a spiritual leader had begun in India in the 1880s, and she established a reputation, both in European and Indian circles, as a wonder-worker even more than as a teacher. It was a time when the physical phenomena of the seance room were very much in the air—the supernatural transportation of material objects, written messages, etc.—and Madame Blavatsky acquired such notoriety in this field that in 1885 the Psychical Research Society sent out a skilled investigator, Richard Hodgson, to look into the matter. He came back with a devastating report. The messages from the Mahatmas, Madame Blavatsky's unseen Masters, were written by herself. Their miraculous transportation was a piece of simple trickery. The shrine at Adyar, the centre of so many remarkable occurrences, turned out to have a sliding panel in the back through which apports from the beyond could be introduced. And so on; the whole sordid repertoire of credulity and fraud.

Madame Blavatsky transferred her operations to London in 1885. Her followers were deeply indignant at the SPR report; indeed most of the faithful had not read it but relied on scandalised hearsay. Yeats had read it, and his attitude towards it is puzzling. He boggled a little at the declaration of allegiance demanded of aspirant members, but by some careful casuistry, at which he was remarkably adept, he contrived to interpret it in such a way as to reconcile it with his conscience. As for the identity of Madame's unseen teachers, he saw four possibilities: they were (1) as HPB said, living occultists; (2) unconscious dramatisations, trance personalities of HPB herself; (3) possibly, but not likely, spirits; (4) the trance principle of nature expressing itself symbolically. And he added, quite firmly, 'The fraud theory in its most pronounced form I have never held for more than a few minutes, as it is wholly unable to cover the facts.' From this I think we can make three deductions. Firstly, that Yeats firmly believed in the value, interest and validity of communications beyond the rational intellect, whether they come from hidden teachers, the unconscious of a medium, or in some way from the collective unconscious. Secondly, this is combined with a fair degree of scepticism about the professed explanation of such messages. Thirdly, in saying he dismissed the fraud theory in its most pronounced form he seems pretty clearly to be suggesting that he entertained it in a less pronounced form. But it does not appear to have worried him in the least. He had an enormous appreciation of Madame Blavatsky as a 'character', some grotesque figure out of Dickens or Balzac. He felt a cheerful contempt for some of the other Theosophists —he described one of them as having the intellect of a good-sized whelk—and he combined this with the complete conviction that something of great importance was nevertheless coming through. This testifies to an attitude Yeats was to retain throughout his life: if you want to explore the shadow side, the hidden channels of human experience, you must be prepared to keep bad company—indeed it is in what the world of scholarship and organised intelligence would call bad company that the deepest mysteries are most likely to be discovered.

And what Yeats actually found in the Theosophical Society was, as I have suggested, virtually the whole of the occultist creed, in a confused and voluminous form. He found the idea of an age-old secret doctrine, passed on by oral tradition from generation to generation. He found a God seen only as the boundless Absolute, impassible, unknowable, indescribable. He found a world consisting of emanations from this Absolute, and souls who were sparks or separated fragments of the same substance. Their object is to return to the One from which they came, but to accomplish this they have to make a long pilgrimage through many incarnations, live through many lives both in this world and beyond. Yeats accepts all this as his natural heritage; it is indeed common doctrine, to be found in Hinduism or Buddhism or Neoplatonism and its offshoots, to all of which Madame Blavatsky claimed kinship. There is no evidence that he paid close attention to the elaborate cosmological symbolism of the Theosophists. Even in youth he was always sophisticated enough to realise that such formulas are of necessity arbitrary, contrived expressions of the inherently inexpressible, and later he was to decide that if there was to be any arbitrary symbolism he would devise his own. In Hindu thought, followed by the Theosophists, reincarnation is in-dissolubly linked to the idea of karma, or destiny—the fate of the soul in incarnation is rigorously determined by its actions in past lives. Yeats never seems to have paid much attention to the grimly retributive aspects of this doctrine; indeed he speaks much about the forgiveness of sins, which to Madame Blavatsky was an unworthy sentimentalisation of the actual laws of the

universe. And it must also be said, I think, both of
Yeats and the Theosophists, that because the One is so
infinitely remote, so radically unapproachable, it
actually arouses less interest than the subordinate
powers who are closer to human life.

Certain principles peculiar to Theosophy seem to
have been of lasting importance to Yeats, and recur
when he came to formulate his own system late in life.
One is the idea of two alternating phases in the self-
unfolding of the One—active and passive, objective
and subjective; called in *Isis Unveiled* 'the days and
nights of Brahma'. With very little change this plays a
central role in the psychology and cosmology of *A
Vision*. Equally important is the elaborately worked-
out doctrine that the incarnations succeed each other in
a determined round. Room is allowed for the variations
of individual destiny, for delays and backslidings en
route; but every soul, every race, and humanity itself,
has an allotted pilgrimage to perform; and this
pilgrimage is part of the structure of the universe. The
element of determinism that so many students of Yeats
have found repugnant in his system seems to have its
root in the Theosophical studies of his very early days.
A more general debt is the pervasive conviction that
any symbolism, however alien and bizarre, any doctrinal
formulation, however hard to assimilate, may be a
fragmentary glimpse of a truth that can never be fully
expressed. In Madame Blavatsky's writing this tendency
runs riot; but tempered by literary tact and poetic
sensibility it is not absent from Yeats.

Yeats was not completely satisfied by the unstrenuous
attitudes and the miscellaneous membership of the

Theosophical Society, and in 1888 he joined the newly-formed Esoteric Section of the London Lodge, an inner circle purposing to devote itself to a more intense and vigorous pursuit of the mysteries. Yeats had a restless and enquiring mind, and from the start was inclined to upset his fellows by pushing his enquiries further than they wanted to go. What is more, he was not interested in joining a seminar or a discussion group; if the unseen world was a source of power, he wanted to lay his hands on it. The Faustian magus, not the devout disciple, represented his secret ideal. Clairvoyance, vision, the summoning of apparitions, were perpetual objects of fascination to him. Among the Theosophists the acquisition and exercise of supernormal faculties, while theoretically admitted, was regarded as in rather bad taste. 'Phenomena' as they were called, were under a cloud—naturally after the Psychical Research society report; and the phenomena of trance and mediumship were always strongly opposed by Madame Blavatsky. Yeats's tireless experimentalism became a cause of scandal in the society, and in 1890 he was asked to resign. This did not however leave him without occult resources, for he had already in the same year joined another society more in tune with his real needs—the Hermetic Order of the Golden Dawn.

The Order of the Golden Dawn was to become the most famous of the magical societies of the turn of the century. It had been founded only a year before, in 1889, by three occult students who were already members of a Rosicrucian society—the Societas Rosicruciana in Anglia. All were Master Masons, which suggests a link with the eighteenth-century

Masonic and Rosicrucian societies of Germany and France, though the Masonic connection had now been dropped. The stimulus to the Golden Dawn was the discovery (or manufacture) of a manuscript in cypher apparently containing fragments of an occult ritual. The most energetic of the three founders was one McGregor Mathers, of whom we hear much in Yeats's autobiographies; he worked on and developed the material in the manuscript, ultimately developing it into an entire ceremonial system. The importance of this is that there was no credo or statement of belief as such; all was implicit in the ritual.

The history of the Golden Dawn has been exhaustively traced by Ellic Howe, and Yeats's relations with it by G.M. Harper.[1] It is not an edifying story. The claims on which the Order was founded were, to put it mildly, fictitious—more bluntly, fraudulent; its operations were marked by wrangles and dissensions, so obsessive and acrimonious as to border on the psychotic. Yet for the twelve years from his initiation to 1902, the ideals and conduct of the Order were of passionate concern to Yeats—besides his poetry the central interest of his life. The basic religious philosophy of the Golden Dawn— its theology, metaphysics and cosmology—was very similar to that of the Theosophical Society. Indeed for a time there were some who belonged to both organisations. But there were important differences. The symbolism, imagery and linguistic resources of the Golden Dawn were drawn from Western sources— Cabalistic and Rosicrucian mainly, with a mass of lesser borrowings from European magical treatises of various periods. The office-bearers in the Golden

Dawn ceremonies have names taken from the Eleusinian mysteries—Hierophant, Dadouchos etc.; Madame Blavatsky's profusion of Sanscrit borrowings do not appear at all, but there are fragmentary quotations in Latin, Greek, Hebrew, and occasionally what I take to be Egyptian. There is plenty of exoticism in the activity of the Golden Dawn, but its catchment area does not extend much beyond the boundaries of the late classical world. There are respectful references to the Christian Cabala, and some of the disciples of the Golden Dawn professed their adherence to Esoteric Christianity—as contrasted with the Theosophists' Esoteric Buddhism; but the infusions of Christian symbolism are slight, and they have to take their place in the eclectic miscellany on equal terms with the rest. A risen saviour may be hailed equally as Christ or as Osiris.

The Theosophical Society was open to all; its teachings were public and published. The Golden Dawn was essentially a secret society. Membership was restricted, supposedly to the duly qualified, and after admission advancement in the society was strictly controlled. It was called an 'order', like a monastic order or an order of chivalry, and in theory at least was bound together by a far more close-knit sense of common purpose than the Theosophists. It was from this time on that the word 'magic' makes its appearance in Yeats's vocabulary, not as a vaguely poetic usage, but as a technical term, meaning the systematic pursuit of occult powers. Rather later in his Golden Dawn career in 1901, Yeats made a formal statement of his magical beliefs:

The Mystery Religion of W.B. Yeats

I believe in the practice and philosophy of what we have agreed to call magic, in what I must call the evocation of spirits, though I do not know what they are, in the power of creating magical illusions, in the visions of truth in the depths of the mind when the eyes are closed; and I believe in three doctrines, which have, as I think, been handed down from early times and been the foundations of nearly all magical practices. These doctrines are

(1) That the borders of our minds are ever shifting, and that many minds can flow into one another, as it were, and create or reveal a single mind, a single energy.

(2) That the borders of our memories are as shifting, and that our memories are part of one great memory, the memory of Nature herself.

(3) That this great mind and great memory can be evoked by symbols.

(E & I 28)

Let us for a moment forswear the seductions of Yeats's enchanting style, and ask in deliberately neutral language what this statement means. It means first a belief in the power of reverie, intensified to such a point that it produces images. These images can become so real that they amount to visions, and the visions can acquire a strength and an autonomy that causes them to be, or to seem to be, independent powers, spirits acting by their own volition; though Yeats is careful to add 'I do not know what they are'. What is more, these visions can be deliberately induced, and a method is

44

named by which it can be done; they can be evoked by symbols. The visions are not confined to the individual mind—they can be shared. This implies in the first place telepathy, as it is ordinarily understood by experimental psychical research, but more specifically, for Yeats and his friends of the Golden Dawn, it implied the power of a disciplined and like-minded group to pool its psychic energies and share its image-making experiences. This has long been the practice of charismatic religious groups and in recent years has also been the subject of experimental research.

So far we are pretty well within the realm of the empirically verifiable. That such experiences occur, and that they can be induced, is not seriously in doubt. The commonsense view would be that such visions, induced by meditation or directed reverie, are simply the products of individual fantasy. But Yeats's confession of faith makes quite a different claim. It is that by these means men can gain access to the great mind, the great memory, that animates the whole universe. This great mind is the World-Soul of the Platonists, the Akasha or Astral Light of Theosophy and, it would seem, the collective unconscious of Jung—an idea that hovers uncertainly between metaphysics and psychology, and claims a foothold alike in mystical intuition, cosmographical speculation and anthropological fact.

The last enigmatic sentence of the Yeatsian creed is that the great mind can be evoked by symbols. Appearing as it does among Yeats's early essays we are apt to interpret the use of 'symbol' here in a literary way; we think of symbolist poetry, of the luminous haze around an inaccessible flame that is so often invoked in the writing of this period. But if we do so we are wrong. Turn to the actual practice of the Golden Dawn, and of Yeats himself as described in his own writing, and we find that 'symbols' are something much more concrete. They are actual shapes, colours, diagrams and manufactured objects, and it was by physical and mental concentration on these specified forms that access to the Great Memory was to be obtained. One of the practices that acquired great popularity among Golden Dawn members was meditation on what were called the Tattva symbols, apparently of Hindu origin. These were simple geometrical forms symbolising the elements—a yellow square for earth, a blue circle for air, a red triangle for fire and a silver crescent for water; and there was actually a fifth, a black oval for the ether. By gazing at one of them fixedly until an after-image was left on the retina, by imagining this as a doorway and passing through it, a train of subsequent imagery could be produced, and this was supposed to give access to the nature and the power of the element concerned and give rise to appropriate visions. With the instinct for elaboration that the Golden Dawn invariably displayed, it was also possible to superimpose one symbol on another—a small red triangle of fire on the yellow square of earth—thus harmonising the participant with the fiery aspect of earth. Other symbols were derived from the traditional magical repertoire—the pentagram or five-pointed star, the six-pointed star or seal of Solomon, and many others, each having special virtues. These figures could not be bought ready-made, so the spiritual life under Golden Dawn auspices involved a good deal of drawing and colouring and cutting out and sticking together. Much use was made of the Tarot cards, those evocative images clearly of some symbolic significance, but given by occultists a weight and a bearing that they were never intended to carry.

Though it is not familiar to us as a religious practice, it can easily be understood that concentrated meditation on visual images of this kind, especially if practised with like-minded companions and with a directed sense of what was to be expected, could produce definite psychic results—mind-pictures; in the sensitive and fantasy-prone, actual visions. But more is claimed for the symbols than that. Meditation on one of the elemental symbols is supposed to lead not only along a mental, an imaginative track, but to a participation in the power of the actual element concerned. There is a vital link between the psychic and the physical realm. As above, so below. And the symbols themselves are not mere programmes for psychic exercises, they are part of the real forces that govern the world. We find Yeats writing, in one of his most deeply felt essays on occult matters:

> It is a first principle of our illumination that symbols and formulae are powers, which act in their own right and with little consideration for our intentions, however excellent. Most of us have seen some ceremony produce an altogether unintended result because of the accidental use of some wrong formula or symbol.[2]

And here I think we come to a parting of ways. The uncommitted observer can comprehend the function of symbols as instigators of meditation, as part of a discipline of the will and the imagination—comparable to the Spiritual Exercises of St Ignatius or the parallel practices of many religious sects. But to believe that the symbolic apparatus acts by its own virtue, *ex opere operato*, is a very different matter, a much bigger pill to swallow. Yet this belief was central to the Golden Dawn, and often reiterated by Yeats. The central and special activity of the Golden Dawn was 'ceremonial magic', a practice pursued with the greatest solemnity by its adherents, but described by others, even by other occultists, as a grotesque and empty charade. If we want to view it in any sort of sympathetic light we must approach it by way of symbol. We can see that symbols can form the objects of meditation, and we may believe that they can lead to visionary experience. Symbols can be drawn, painted, physically gazed at or imagined in the mind's eye; and they can also be enacted. And this of course is what religious ceremonial is—an enacted symbol. Long usage and density of association may give it great power. But more recent, deliberately devised ceremonies are without that source of strength, and remain thin and one-dimensional in consequence. It could hardly have been otherwise with the rituals of the Golden Dawn—apart from the defects of Mathers' liturgical style. It is clear that they were felt to be deeply significant by their participants, but to the outside observer they are fatally lacking in resonance and depth, and it is surely impossible to believe in their having any intrinsic efficacy.

They are mostly rituals of initiation. The organisation of the Golden Dawn was based on a system of grades. The candidate enters as a Neophyte and gradually works his way up through the ranks of Theoricus, Practicus. Minor Adept and Major Adept towards the status of a full-blown Magus. The candidate is tested by quite severe examinations at every stage, and the ceremonials set the seal on his attainment of a particular stage of spiritual development. In some ways being in the Golden Dawn must have been very like being in the Boy Scouts of my childhood; you were always working for badges. Like it also in that ambitions were on the whole limited. Nobody one actually knew ever got beyond Second-Class Scout; so in the Golden Dawn the ordinary member was not expected to go beyond the grade of Minor Adept; those who rose higher than this were either rare and exceptional persons or not in the flesh at all, pure spirits; and the incarnate leaders of the Order professed to receive their authority from spiritual masters in these higher realms. The system of grades first makes its appearance in a Rosicrucian society in eighteenth-century Germany, and there is of course an analogue in freemasonry, from which indeed this allegedly Rosicrucian system may be derived. There seems something slightly absurd in such anxious exam-passing, and the impression is not lessened when we inspect the curriculum—learning the Hebrew alphabet, the signs of the Zodiac and how to draw pentagrams. But we should try to rid ourselves of these ludicrous associations, for here the grade system leads on to something much more important. In the Golden Dawn the ten grades were equated with the ten emanatory spheres of the Hebrew Cabala. In speaking of the general character of occultist creeds we found that they tended to abandon the idea of divine creation, and replace it by the idea of successive emanations from the ineffable One. The Cabala has a doctrine of this kind, and the ten emanations are called the Sephiroth. They are arranged in a diagrammatic pattern called the Tree of Life, which can be seen either as the descent of power from the Godhead to the lower world, or as the ascent from the lowest sphere, the material world in which we live, to the divine. And it is this latter process, the ascent from the material world to the divine, that is, we are to suppose, not merely symbolised, but actualised by progress through the Golden Dawn grades.

There is much in Golden Dawn practice that is arbitrary, much that is absurd; but this central complex diagram of the Tree of Life stands clear of all the inferior material. We have first to accustom ourselves to the idea that profound insights into the nature of man and his relation with the world can be expressed in symbol and diagram as well as in theological argument and credal assertion. We can then begin to realise that each of the ten Sephiroth is itself a symbol of great richness and depth, and can be equated with other symbols from many fields of myth, religious philosophy and quasi-scientific speculation. The second and third Sephiroth, for example, seem to be identical with the Yang and the Yin, the male and female principle, of Chinese philosophy. The seventh, eighth, ninth and tenth are closely analogous to the four faculties—thought, feeling, intuition and sensation—of Jungian psychology. The original Hebrew titles of the Sephiroth were attributes of God—glory, wisdom, mercy, beauty, etc. But the gods of the ancient world can also find their place upon the tree, Olympians and Egyptian deities alike. The sixth Sephira is the sphere of harmony and reconciliation; also of sacrifice. It is here that redeemers and sacrificed gods belong, and it is here that modern Cabalists find their link with Christianity.

Striking analogies can be found too with the concepts of astrology and alchemy—trivial if they are regarded as failed sciences but significant if they are looked at as projections of psychic contents. The Sephiroth were identified with the alchemical metals and with the stars—most importantly with the seven planets. The addition of the Primum Mobile, the sphere of the fixed stars and the sublunary sphere of the elements, brings the number up to the required ten. Hebrew cosmology had already described the planets not as dead stars but as living beings, as archangels whose brilliance was a celebration of the glory of God. And for the West the planets were already identified by name and nature with the ancient gods—Venus, Mercury, Sun, Moon and the rest. So that for syncretist students of the Cabala from the Renaissance to modern occultism the whole range of pagan symbolism was brought into the system—remote as that was from the intentions of the devout rabbis who devised it. It is thus possible to see, behind the bewildering accumulation of lists, spells, exotic nomenclature and incantation with which the Golden Dawn snowed up its neophytes, the outline of a system of correspondences which is in principle capable of absorbing the religions of the

51

world, because it goes deeper than the particulars of any of them, down to their psychic roots.

In short, what we are offered by these central Cabalistic presuppositions of the Golden Dawn is a sort of ground-plan, a skeleton outline, on which an immense range of myth, religion and speculative philosophy can be projected. The value of this to Yeats was inestimable. From childhood on he had been assembling a miscellany of legendary material from which he hoped to extract a philosophy of life. Here he found an organising principle capable of bringing all together, capable too of satisfying both sides of his nature—the propensity to dream, and to expand his dream until it included everything; and the other propensity, much less noted in commentary on Yeats, to systematise, to order, to bring all the vagaries of reverie under a single rule. The impulse that lies behind this endeavour finds other expressions around the turn of the century. It is this that led George Eliot's Mr Casaubon to project a key to all the mythologies, and Sir James Frazer actually to provide one. It lies behind the Jungian psychology too, and is not absent even from the apparent positivism and scientism of Freud. It is the drive, by no means exhausted even today, to find beneath the bewildering variety of images and concepts in which men have expressed their sense of their own being and their relation to the gods, a level of interpretation that would be valid for all. To the psychologists and anthropologists this is a critical enquiry; to occultists and aspirant magicians it is an existential plunge into a shoreless sea. But this, it must be confessed, is an interpretation of the Golden Dawn softened by distance and hindsight. At closer range the farrago of absurdities, the frequent injections of sheer superstitious nonsense, is apt to obscure the view.

Yeats's deepest commitment to the Golden Dawn is recorded in a paper presented to the governing body of the Order itself, during the most serious of its periodical crises of organisation, in 1901.[3] It is a ten-page essay, partly indeed dealing with administrative wrangles, but in much larger part concerned with what Yeats felt to be the true inner meaning of Golden Dawn activities, and written with deep feeling. In it he writes 'A Magical Order differs from a society for experiment and research in that it is an actual Being, an organic life holding within itself the highest life of its members.' There can be no doubt that Yeats regarded the Golden Dawn as a mystic community, and though deeply concerned with its backsliding and failures in precise observance, he was not in the least inclined to criticise its premises or its chosen symbolism, however bizarre and arbitrary. However, the other side of the coin represented in the sentence just quoted—'experiment and research'—was also very much part of Yeats's nature. The Golden Dawn practice of meditating on symbols was used by Yeats, not only in its primary function as a stimulus to visionary experience, but also as a means of experimenting in thought transmission. Both with his uncle George Pollexfen and with Maud Gonne he attempted, by contemplating a particular symbol, to cause an appropriate vision to arise in his partner's mind, and these attempts were often success-ful. On the fringe of the Golden Dawn's quasi-mystical and religious preoccupations there was always, as far as

53

Yeats was concerned, a good deal of sheer experimental curiosity.

This is something we associate with the quasi-scientific pursuits of the Society for Psychical Research rather than with the occultist pathways frequented by Yeats. His attitude was different from that of the psychical researchers in that it was determined by an initial conviction of the reality of a spiritual world. But he shared with them a quite positive and undoctrinal belief that the mind had hidden powers, and that investigation of them was a prime avenue to a world of psychic activity normally concealed from view. Yeats saw, as some psychical researchers have failed to see, that the mere fact of telepathy, non-sensory communication from mind to mind—if it should prove to be a fact—is sufficient to upset the mechanist-materialist suppositions on which the everyday notions of the modern world are based. He would have found little to disapprove of in the modern card-guessing experiments, as a means of exploring the working and the limits of the extra-sensory faculties. For all his hospitality to the supernatural, the sceptical and inquiring strain in him was strong. From very early days, when such sophistication was rare, he displayed a well-informed awareness of the nature of seance-room communications and their liability to be taken over by secondary personalities of the medium. Though indulgent to old-wives' tales, he was acutely aware of the possibilities of deliberate fraud. In 1914, for example, we find him collaborating with Everard Feilding, a prominent member of the SPR, in investigating a supposedly miraculous holy picture at Mirebeau near Poitiers; and coming eventually to the conclusion that it was a deception. And this was only one of many such investigations in which Yeats was involved.

More central to his concerns was mediumship, which at the height of his enthusiasm he was willing to pursue in any quarter, reputable or disreputable—for it offered to provide a direct contact with the spirit world. In his later years Yeats became increasingly preoccupied with the question of survival and a life after death, and any avenue, however unlikely, that seemed to afford a glimpse into it was welcome to him. He had his first experience of a spiritualist seance in 1886, in Dublin. He found that he had nearly fallen into trance, was considerably shaken by the experience, and for years afterwards would take no part in such activities. Both the Theosophists and the Golden Dawn were strongly opposed to mediumship, on the grounds that it was a merely *passive* process—while it was the business of the occult adept to assume command of the psychic powers. And it was not until the years preceding the Great War, when his attachment to the Golden Dawn had considerably relaxed, that mediumship again began to occupy him seriously. It was part of a general movement of his interests from ritual and ceremonial magic to what could almost be called spiritualism in the ordinarily accepted sense. Not quite, however; for what to the thoroughgoing spiritualist was a matter of religious faith was to Yeats still subject to investigation. He says at one point that he was not concerned with 'evidence of the kind the Society for Psychical Research would value'; but as a matter of fact he was. From 1911 to 1914 he was deeply engaged in investigations on

55

precisely the SPR model. And he came to positive conclusions. He claims at last to have 'proved spirit identity', and to be in possession of evidence that the Psychical Research Society would acknowledge: and later in life Dorothy Wellesley reports him as saying 'Individual immortality is proved now beyond a doubt; there is sufficient evidence to prove it again and again in a court of law.'

Yeats's renewed interest in mediumship and the phenomena of the seance-room dates from 1911, when he met a currently celebrated medium 'Mrs C' (Mrs Chenoweth) in Boston. On his return from America he began to attend seances in London with a number of different mediums, and the surviving records make it abundantly clear that his interest was deep and sustained. His two principal mediums were Mrs Wreidt, an American from Detroit, and Miss Radcliffe, an English girl. Both produced copious messages from a variety of communicators, sometimes polyglot, in languages with which it is said the mediums were not acquainted. The main theoretical interest of these seances was in the proof of spirit identity. To quote Flournoy, one of the most sober and established of psychic investigators, whom we know Yeats to have read:

> There is nothing against the idea that we might give the name "spirit" to an unknown psychic complex which unites into one whole a plurality of psychic ideas, states, and feelings below the threshold of consciousness. . . . The question is, whether this "psychic self" is really external to the

56

medium (as spiritists assert), or whether it is not within herself, and the personality which manifested in these messages was not a purely temporary function—a projection or momentary creation of her being—such as the creations of our dreams, with which we speak and hold conversations.

Flournoy had no doubt of the answer—the 'spirits' were aspects of the medium's mind, perhaps telepathically induced by incursions from the minds of the investigators. But to Yeats, as indeed to many other serious enquirers up to the present day, this explanation raised more difficulties than it solved. Starting from the premiss that the spirits might be what they said they were he made prolonged and pertinacious researches in public records, works of reference and so forth, to confirm their own accounts of themselves. In this he had some successes. These 'drop-in communicators' as modern psychical researchers label them, who seem indeed to appear out of the blue for no particular reason, did in some cases turn out to be real people, whose existence and past histories could be independently confirmed. But as usual, there were loopholes; the confirmations all fell short of certainty, and though exciting at the time, in retrospect the seance material was tantalising and disappointing. The most important visitant to Yeats's seances was one Leo Africanus, who appeared repeatedly, professed to be Yeats's *alter ego*, his opposite, a sort of complementary attendant daimon. This was a conception which came to have great importance for Yeats, fulfilling much the same role as the 'inferior function' in Jungian psychology, that area of the psyche that lies buried in the unconscious and that must be recovered if wholeness of being is to be achieved. But Leo Africanus, it turned out, was a historical character, a Moorish traveller of the sixteenth century who had written a famous description of Africa. When Yeats discovered that he was also a poet he became all the more eager to adopt him as a psychic companion, and the question of whether Leo was the spirit he claimed to be or a mere cultural and psychological artefact continued to exercise him for some time.

There is nearly always something faded and uncompelling about the mere reports of seance-room experiences, and Yeats's are no exception. Happily however we have also a document of another kind, the rich and brilliant essay 'Swedenborg, Mediums and the Desolate Places' (E 30–73), written in 1914, in which Yeats sums up and contemplates his psychic experiences of the past few years. He was not squeamish in his researches, and they included, besides the mediums with some intellectual pretensions, a good many more humble soothsayers in Holloway and Soho. These excursions carried his mind back to his folklore activities of fifteen years before, when he had gone from cottage to cottage with Lady Gregory, collecting stories and legends. He soon began to find among modern town-bred spiritualists, especially the uneducated ones, beliefs that were identical with those of the Galway peasantry. He was not, he says, so much searching for 'evidence' in the SPR sense, as comparing one belief with another, looking for a common substratum of doctrine about an objectively existing spirit world. He read all the reputable modern

works on the subject that he could find in English or
French, both quasi-scientific and overtly spiritualist—
Flournoy, Myers, Aksakoff, but also Alan Kardec
and Jackson Davies—excited, stimulated, but always
reserving final judgment. Then in 1914 he read
Swedenborg, or rather re-read him, for he had looked
at some of his writings without special attention or
interest years before. The *Spiritual Diary* and *Heaven
and Hell* are the relevant works: and here Yeats found,
set out in a chill schematic style, like a traveller's report,
a description of the spirit world exactly corresponding
to that which had come through in folk tales and
communications of the seance-room.

The testimony of Swedenborg was made impressive
to Yeats by its radically prosaic, unimaginative nature.
Not only was Swedenborg a scientist, he was essentially
a taxonomist, a classifier, who treated the phenomena
observed in his visions of the spirit world exactly as
he treated his specimens of minerals. Yet it was
Swedenborg, in Yeats's words, who 'affirmed for the
modern world, as against the abstract reasoning of the
learned, the doctrine and practice of the desolate
places, of shepherds and midwives, and discovered a
world of spirits where there was a scenery like that of
earth, human forms, grotesque or beautiful, senses that
knew pleasure and pain, marriage and war, all that
could be painted upon canvas, or put into stories to
make one's hair stand up.' (E.32) From Swedenborg
Yeats's essay passes on to Blake, from Blake to modern
spiritualists, and from them to the Noh plays of Japan,
with their plots about hauntings and restless ghosts.
All, in differing formulations, seem to bear the same

witness, of a different kind from that he had found in the occult societies, not the results of reverie and meditation but reports, descriptions, of another world objectively existing, where the spirits of the dead live on, a continuation of their earthly existence, and mingle with other spirits who perhaps had never lived human lives.

All this takes us a long way from the aspirations of Pythagoreans, Platonists or world-forsaking Indians. A little later than the Swedenborg essay Yeats wrote the obscure, profound and beautiful *Per Amica Silentia Lunae*, and a little later still began the mediumistic experiences that led to the compilation of *A Vision*. Here we enter difficult territory, and the landscape seems to change bewilderingly as we pass through it; but what we see constantly as we become accustomed to these changed surroundings is that the spirit world is less unfamiliar than we might have supposed; it comes more and more to resemble an apotheosis of the world of sense. In the succession of incarnations and the active, populated spaces between them the flight of the Alone to the Alone seems indefinitely postponed.

III. Magic and Poetry

We have now reached the time when the materials of Yeats's religious philosophy had all been assembled. Up to this point his attitude to them had been largely receptive. He had given hospitality to a great variety of symbolisms, without feeling the need for making any exact synthesis between them. Theosophy, the system of the Golden Dawn and Spiritualism, were not exactly coincident but they were not discordant either, and his researches in mythology and folklore repeatedly assured him that they were all moving along the same road. The Cabalistic scheme of the Sephiroth, the Tree of Life, encouraged this way of thinking, for it is a kind of ground-plan on which all the mythologies of the world can be projected. But in the end of course Yeats did make his own synthesis, and we have the result in that remarkable work *A Vision*, in its two versions, one of 1925 and one of 1937.

The story of its origin is well known. A few days after his marriage in 1917 Yeats's wife surprised him by attempting automatic writing. The fragmentary messages that came through were arresting. Yeats encouraged her to continue; and soon they came to seem of the deepest significance. The 'unknown communicators' seemed to be doing little less than dictating a whole philosophy of life and death. Yeats was so stirred and excited by this that he offered to devote the remainder of his life to ordering and expounding the message. The communicators forbade this. They said 'we come to give you metaphors for poetry'. But the messages continued, and 'the system', as he often called it, dominated Yeats's imagination for the last twenty years of his life. Now whatever mysteries may remain in the doctrine and imagery of this system—and to me there are still many, not to mention a good deal of muddle—the mysterious nature of its genesis can be considerably toned down. In the course of his fifty years Yeats had accumulated a vast farrago of myth and symbolism. Much of this remained external to him. He needed now to make it more fully his own. The things said by the unknown communicators were very much the same *sort* of things Yeats had been hearing and saying all his life. And as for the part played by Mrs Yeats—she was a fellow member of the Golden Dawn, and had already been a collaborator in occult explorations. What came through is clearly quite beyond the possibilities of conscious co-production; but automatic writing is a classic field for telepathic fusion. Quasi-unconscious communal productions of this kind are numerous in the annals of physical research. Yeats himself said 'Much that has happened, much that has been said, suggests that the communicators are the personalities of a dream shared by my wife, by myself, occasionally by others'. As for the identity of the 'others', Yeats believed quite positively in collaboration between the living and the dead; and that is a matter whose possibility the ignorant will settle out of hand according to their previous convictions. Those who have taken the trouble to go into these matters mostly confess that they have to leave it undecided.

What can be quite easily decided is that *A Vision* is not a transcription of the automatic writings. The first published version appeared in 1925—that is to say it had been seven years on the stocks. In it Yeats talks about 'the notes on which I have based this book', and says in another place 'the documents are very confused, and what I have written is less based upon what they say than upon my knowledge of the system as a whole.' It is quite clear therefore that *A Vision* is not a dictated text, it is an artefact. Its symbolism is unique and original, but it is similar in kind and owes much in substance to the elaborate and multifarious symbolic systems that Yeats had been brooding over for many years, and much to research and deliberate art. We would be mistaken, I believe, to regard it as a sourcebook for the later poetry, a key to a cypher. It is a work of imagination; it is itself poetry—but poetry of a different kind from any that Yeats had written before.

A Vision is in an established literary mode. It is an apocalypse, a revelation, with most of the characteristics that belong to such literature—riddling or fictional or visionary introductions; claims to universality which go uneasily with fragmentariness and incompleteness; a gnomic and authoritative manner; strange or baffling assertions put down without argument or support; symbolism that partly belongs to the common cultural stock, but suddenly becomes enigmatic or incomprehensible. The type for our literature is the biblical Apocalypse, so overwhelming that it seems to stand alone. But the same genre is to be seen in the visions of Daniel and Ezekiel, in Boehme's *Aurora, The Marriage of Heaven and Hell*, Poe's *Eureka, Thus Spake Zarathustra* and the *Fantasia of the Unconscious*. Maddening from the point of view of science or professional philosophy, such works are rarely satisfying from the aesthetic point of view either, but they exercise enormous and disconcerting power. In Yeats's case it is a power of attraction that causes all the other work of his later years to cluster round this revelation at a greater or less distance.

Yeats takes for granted the conception of the destiny of the human soul that we have found common to the occult tradition. Indeed he takes it so much for granted that he scarcely finds it necessary to state it; and a good deal of the bewilderment that faces the unprepared reader of *A Vision* comes simply because the fundamentals of its creed are never explicitly set out. They are quite definite, however and may take several forms; the form they take in Yeats is inherited from Madame Blavatsky. It is stated very clearly in a passage of her *Key to Theosophy*:

> Try to imagine a 'spirit', a celestial Being, divine in its essential nature, yet not pure enough to be *one with the* ALL, and having, in order to achieve this, so to purify its nature as finally to gain that goal. It can only do so by passing *individually* and

personally, i.e., physically and spiritually, through every experience and feeling that exists in the manifold and differentiated Universe. It has, therefore, . . . to pass through every experience on the human planes.[1]

Yeats's central symbol for this totality, comparable to the Cabalistic Tree of Life, similarly presents itself as a diagram of all the possibilities of human experience. It is a circle called the Great Wheel, divided into twenty-eight segments, pictured as the twenty-eight days of a lunar month. This is rather more than an arbitrary piece of imaginative notation, for it embodies the essential of the system—the polarity between phase 1, the darkness when the moon is occulted, and phase 15, the brilliance of the moon at the full. Yeats calls the dark phase objective or primary; the light is subjective or antithetical. He is never very happy with this terminology, and neither are his readers. The concepts are difficult and only gradually make themselves clear. Unconscious and passive might serve as qualifications for the dark objective, active and self-aware for the subjective light. Between them lie all the potentialities of experience, conceived by Yeats, as by the Theosophists before him, to be successive incarnations which every soul must go through in an ordered round. Not complete determinism, as a frequent accusation against Yeats would have it, for a complicated psychology which we cannot follow here leaves within each incarnation plenty of room for will and choice. But not flitting like a butterfly over random fields of flowers; one phase leads to the next, inexorably. And n the cycle is completed it begins again.

Moving counter-clockwise round the circle man begins in the darkness of phase 1, which also seems to mean materiality or merely physical life, and struggles towards his opposite, the full light of phase 15. During this progress man is struggling with himself; the body is becoming ever more possessed and impregnated by the spirit, and becoming ever more beautiful as it does so. At the full of the moon, when the body is perfectly moulded by the soul, the result is perfect beauty; and this type is too perfect to lie in any earthly cradle. These are daimonic or supernatural beings. In the succeeding phases man begins the return towards objectivity. He struggles with the world instead of with himself. At first he retains the subjective radiance, but as we approach the last quarter the incarnations become dulled and coarsened. The succeeding types are summarised as follows in the poem 'The Phases of the Moon':

> The soul remembering its loneliness
> Shudders in many cradles; all is changed,
> It would be the world's servant, and as it serves,
> Choosing whatever task's most difficult
> Among tasks not impossible, it takes
> Upon the body and upon the soul
> The coarseness of the drudge . . .

> Reformer, merchant, statesman, learned man,
> Dutiful husband, honest wife by turn,
> Cradle upon cradle, and all in flight and all
> Deformed because there is no deformity
> But saves us from a dream. (CP 187)

Until, through the last three types, the Hunchback, the Saint and the Fool, we return to the first phase, the dark of the moon, where the dough is kneaded up again, to be formed anew after the old pattern.

For all its other-worldly origins, a good deal of this is quite mundane and unmetaphysical. Much of it looks like a restatement, with some supernatural panache, of Yeats's normal social and political sentiments. It had always been evident that he would prefer a society of nobles, sages, peasants and lunatics to a society of meritocratic officials and psychiatric social workers. Disregarding their status as successive incarnations, the descriptions of the phases amount in effect to a theory of psychological types; and following the initial revelation Yeats pursued an intensive course of biographical reading to furnish himself with real-life examples. The results are often bizarre and sometimes strangely penetrating. But these are secondary and contingent interests. Essentially the doctrine of the Great Wheel makes a different kind of claim. It claims to reveal a pattern in the real structure of the world. The same rhythm runs through all human activity. The same cycle is traversed in the succession of incarnations, in an individual life, in a single judgment or act of thought. It is the rhythm of every completed act of mind or life. It is also therefore the rhythm of collective life, the rhythm of history. Accordingly the cycle of incarnations in *A Vision* is parallelled by a cyclical pattern in history.

Just how much of this came from the unknown communicators we cannot determine. Any such suggestion fused easily in Yeats's mind with astrological

67

and cosmological ideas already familiar to him—the eras and aeons of Theosophy, the Great Year of the Platonists in which a revolution of the whole stellar system is completed. And stimulated by the revelation Yeats began to read a great deal of history, especially writers with theories of the historical process—Vico, Toynbee, later Spengler himself. The Great Year has been variously calculated; Yeats makes it 26,000 years—too large to have much explanatory value for human history. But it has smaller cycles within it, notably the period of 2000 years in which the sun at the equinox passes through a single zodiacal sign. And each of these can be seen as two cycles of 1000 years. These are the units that Yeats works with. The 2000 years of antique civilisation before the birth of Christ are one full cycle; the near 2000 years from the birth of Christ to our own day are another. Here it is plain that we are at least partly in the realm of mythology, but only partly; for myth is mingled with quite substantial historical propositions. Each cycle is inaugurated by an irruption of the divine into the human; the cycle of antiquity by the rape of Leda by Zeus; our own cycle by the incarnation of Christ; the cycle that is approaching by a deity only darkly foreseen. We begin with a purely mythical prelude. Zeus in the guise of a swan ravishes Leda; Leda begets Helen and so foredooms the Trojan War and all its consequences (CP 241);

> The broken wall, the burning roof and tower
> And Agamemnon dead—

the whole tragic and heroic civilisation of the ancient

world. The end of every cycle is a time of exhaustion, turbulence and destruction. The ancient world wears itself out; an angel announces a new dispensation, and it begins when the Virgin conceives of the Holy Ghost. But even this incarnation is turbulent. The Magi see it as 'the uncontrollable mystery on the bestial floor' (CP 141). It ushers in 'a fabulous formless darkness' that dissolves all the structures of previous civilisation.

> Odour of blood when Christ was slain
> Made all Platonic tolerance vain
> And vain all Doric discipline. (CP 240)

And now, 2000 years later, at the end of the worn-out Christian centuries, the Magi are looking for a new incarnation. All readers of Yeats know how he saw the god of the new age. With bitter irony he uses the hallowed formula of Christian hope and calls it the Second Coming.

> The Second Coming! Hardly are those words out
> When a vast image out of *Spiritus Mundi*
> Troubles my sight: somewhere in sands of the desert
> A shape with lion body and the head of a man,
> A gaze blank and pitiless as the sun,
> Is moving its slow thighs, while all about it
> Reel shadows of the indignant desert birds.
> The darkness drops again; but now I know
> That twenty centuries of stony sleep
> Were vexed to nightmare by a rocking cradle,
> And what rough beast, its hour come round at last,
> Slouches towards Bethlehem to be born? (CP 211)

Yeats died in 1939, so did not live to see the answer to his question—that the desert was Los Alamos, and Bethlehem Hiroshima.

The historical cycles are expounded in an elaborate geometrical symbolism of cones and spirals. Whether some demented Pythagorean ghost was responsible for this, or whether Yeats had merely been reading the *Timaeus* we cannot tell; but I do not believe that this exposition has ever brought anything but confusion, so I will say no more of it. But for all the mystification, as with the psychological types, there is much that is quite mundanely intelligible. The historical cycles are chronologically definable periods. When a cycle ends it does not generate some mysterious replica of itself. The same pattern recurs, but in a different material. The form is determined but the content unpredictable. Yeats's scheme does not face us with the difficulties of Nietzsche's Eternal Return even if, as I suspect, the motives behind them are the same—a denial of Hegelian transcendence that itself becomes a transcendent value. The chronology sometimes becomes difficult, since it cannot be exact and is complicated by the competing scales. What is phase 15, full moon, of the whole 2000 years is the dark phase 28 of the 1000-year cycle. It is also true that the periodicities can only be made to work by a strict geographical selection. While the Athenians are enjoying a glorious cultural fulfilment the Boeotians a few hundred miles to the north may still be wallowing in primeval rusticity. However, in the historical commentary the 1000-year cycles become the more important, and as we approach normally recorded history both the track of a general order and certain brilliantly illuminated patches become clearer. Each 1000-year period has its phases of growth, its culminating period at phase 15, and its phases of decline. We leave mythology and enter history with the millenium before Christ. It has its culminating phase, where unity of being was most nearly possible, in fifth-century Athens. In the thousand years after the birth of Christ the climactic phase is in Byzantium of the fifth century A.D., just before the closing of the Platonic Academy. In the era from the year 1000 to the present day it is in the early Renaissance—in effect quattrocento Florence. The history that is tacitly invoked is almost entirely the history of the arts, and of these cultural high points the one that reverberated most strongly in Yeats's imagination was Byzantium. In one of the most haunting passages of *A Vision* he writes:

> If I could be given a month of Antiquity and leave to spend it where I chose, I would spend it in Byzantium a little before Justinian opened St. Sophia and closed the Academy of Plato. I think I could find in some little wine-shop some philosophical worker in mosaic who could answer all my questions, the supernatural descending nearer to him than to Plotinus even. . . . I think that in early Byzantium, maybe never before or since in recorded history, religious, aesthetic and practical life were one. (VB 279)

And so, by reason it seems of this purely aesthetic consummation, Byzantium becomes a holy city—the holy city, where art and the spiritual life are ultimately

71

fused. In the first of the two Byzantium poems it is set against the life of generation and the natural passions:

The young
In one another's arms, birds in the trees,

the country that old men must abandon. And the spirit of Byzantium is embodied, unalluringly, in an eternal metallic artefact. Although the image comes from the historical part of the Yeatsian system, the connection with the historical Byzantium is of the slightest and when we turn to the second poem, Byzantium has taken leave of the earth altogether and become an unchristian New Jerusalem, an intricate symbol of the initial purgatorial stages of the life beyond the grave. Again, as with the Phases of the Moon and the doctrine of the Opposite or Mask we have a prose account as well as the poem. Book III of *A Vision*, 'The Soul in Judgment' tells of the life of the next world.

The subject had always been of abiding interest to Yeats, and his is only one of many such reports, from the Tibetan Book of the Dead to the Theosophical and Spiritualist documents of recent times. The most notable guide-book in the modern period is Swedenborg's; and Yeats follows fairly closely on Swedenborgian lines—with the difference that what for Swedenborg, who is not a reincarnationist, is a final state, is for Yeats only the interval between death and rebirth. Book III of *A Vision* systematises this elaborately. The main features are a reliving by the spirit, over and over again, of the events that have most moved it in life. This is at first compulsive, and is called the Dreaming Back; later it becomes a voluntary purgation, undertaken that all may be understood, all converted into knowledge. When the spirit has thus exhausted all passionate events, and its intentions have been purified of the 'complexity' of phenomenal life, it is no longer one of 'the dead', but is a free spirit, prepared in due time to pass on to a new round of existence—in Swedenborg the passage to another discarnate plane, in Yeats to a new incarnation. Yeats's delineation is filled with closely specified detail, more precisely and positively rendered even than Swedenborg's, and like Swedenborg's it is largely a repetition of what has already happened in the flesh, a continuation of its passions, and even its relations with other beings. So that the whole myth takes the form of an indefinite extension of the phenomenal world, as though it were that which Yeats wishes to make eternal. The superficially similar Indian cycle of incarnations is filled with the longing to escape from the wheel to a timeless, passionless, changeless state; and though this may have been held up by Yeats as an ultimate goal there are few traces of it in his actual imaginative activity. His father once remarked to him 'your interest is in mundane things, whether beyond the stars or not.' And Yeats could well have endorsed these words of C.G. Jung, contrasting his own position with the oriental one:

> The Indian's goal is the condition of *nirvandva*. He wishes to free himself from nature; in keeping with this aim, he seeks in meditation the condition of imagelessness and emptiness. I, on the other hand, wish to persist in the state of lively

73

contemplation of nature and of the psychic images. I want to be freed neither from human beings, nor from myself, nor from nature; for all these appear to me the greatest of miracles.[2]

It follows from this that although the religious tradition to which Yeats belongs posits as the ultimate goal a condition of union with the divine in which the accidents of human individuality are simply burnt away, this goal is for him so infinitely remote that he does not often turn to it, even in contemplation. It is the lower slopes of the holy mountain that allure his footsteps—just as in popular Neoplatonism it is the daimons, the subordinate powers, that attract most attention, rather than the imageless, passionless, unconditioned One. Many of the poems of the later period, when Yeats was most intensely occupied with the enigmatic pronouncements that led to *A Vision*, take the form of dialogues, debates, between self and soul, sense and spirit, the passionate variety of earthly life and the unity of the life beyond. There are glimpses of the celestial state—one in 'Anima Mundi', a prose essay of 1917, taken up again in a poem fifteen years later, characteristically called 'Vacillation'. Here is the prose version:

> At certain moments, always unforeseen, I become happy. . . . Perhaps I am sitting in some crowded restaurant, [an] open book beside me, or closed, my excitement having overbrimmed the page. I look at the strangers near to me as if I had known them all my life, and it seems strange that I

cannot speak to them; everything fills me with affection; I have no longer any fears or any needs: I do not even remember that this happy mood must come to an end. It seems as if the vehicle had become pure and far extended and so luminous that the images from *Anima Mundi* embodied there, ... would burn up time. It may be an hour before the mood passes, but latterly I seem to understand that I enter upon it the moment I cease to hate. (M 36A)

Yeats calls this state the condition of fire; and imagery of fire and flame marks all his attempts to approach this region. The second Byzantium poem portrays the purgatorial stage by which the condition of blessedness is to be enduringly possessed. It speaks of the soul freeing itself of all complexities, 'the fury and the mire of human veins'. But it then presents a vision of spirit life that is crowded, packed with imagery so dense and so complex that it almost defies exposition. The poem is justly celebrated, for it reaches a pitch of intricacy and intensity that makes it a unique achievement. But it *is* unique. Nowhere else does Yeats make such a decisive attempt to cross the *flammantia moenia mundi*. And the cold flames that light the pavement of Byzantium are not the characteristic illumination of Yeats's spirit world. Far more native to Yeats's imagination is the light that shines on the tomb of Baile and Ailin, the tragic lovers united only in death, whose sexual passion is transfigured into a celestial flame (CP 327). And as the late poetry continues its progress it becomes increasingly clear that when Yeats arrives at the gates of paradise he will have all his sensual baggage with him, to be received and legitimated within the holy city.

Not only are many of the later poems vacillations between sense and spirit, dialogues of self and soul; the tenor of all of them is to redeem bodily and sensuous experience and give it its place in the world of spirit, where it becomes eternal. And if we stand back from *A Vision*, far enough back to lose the detail and see only its situation in the economy of Yeats's thought, we can see that that is its function, to bring together his magical speculations and his worldly experience, not in an antinomian marriage of heaven and hell, like Blake's, but a *hieros gamos*, a marriage of heaven and earth in which every feeling or event, from the highest to the lowest, has its own rights and its proper place.

With this in mind we can begin to ask the question that most readers of Yeats will certainly want to ask: How is all this occultist activity, whose scope and intensity we cannot doubt, related to the poetry? How does it appear in the poetry? And how is it that so many readers have formed their view of the poetry in relative innocence of all this formidable background? We have several answers to this group of questions. We have the answer suggested by Auden: the occult beliefs are a regrettable aberration, an astonishing personal folly that runs on beside the poetry (poetry whose greatness Auden does not seem to doubt) but leaves it unaffected. This cannot be true. We have the answer of the professed initiates, like F.A.C. Wilson: Yeats's occult learning provided him with a symbolical cypher that we have to interpret—reading Yeats is a kind of code-breaking. This could be true, and a great deal of strenuous endeavour has gone into turning Yeats's poetry into this kind of *trobar clus*; but the results produced by it are too crabbed and meagre to be adequate to our sense of what Yeats really stands for. And we have the answers provided by critics who are themselves speculative metaphysicians, and regard all Yeats's writing as a text for exposition, to be judged by its doctrinal soundness.

Behind these views—Auden's dismissal, the varied exegetical labours, lies. the assumption that Yeats's poetry should provide an alternative statement of his speculative philosophy, a translation into images of the hermetic conceptual scheme. But in fact we find this very rarely, and late in Yeats's career. In the years from 1890 to 1900, when he was engaged most intensely with the profuse and intricate symbolical system of the Golden Dawn, hardly any of it appears directly in the poetry; and what little does appear is fleeting, wandering and displaced. In 1889, when Yeats was still engaged with the Dublin Hermetic Society, an emissary of Madame Blavatsky, one Mohini Chatterjee appeared in Dublin and deeply fascinated this band of juvenile occultists. They asked him if they should pray, and he replied that prayer was too full of hope and desire to be the true road to wisdom. Yeats turned his words into what he later describes as 'clumsy verse'—a poem called 'Kanva on Himself', included in *The Wanderings of Oisin*. It was indeed not very distinguished verse, and was dropped from the *Collected Poems*. But the idea in it was vital, and thirty-five years later Yeats took

77

it up again, with all the authority of his later manner, in the poem called 'Mohini Chatterjee', written in 1929.

> I asked if I should pray,
> But the Brahmin said,
> 'Pray for nothing, say
> Every night in bed,
> 'I have been a king,
> I have been a slave,
> Nor is there anything,
> Fool, rascal, knave,
> That I have not been,
> And yet upon my breast
> A myriad heads have lain.'   (CP 279)

This is central to Yeats's creed in more than one way; in the total absence of any sense of a personal God to whom prayer could be addressed, or who could be reached by entreaty; in the belief in a plurality of lives, of reincarnation; and in the implied belief that the individual, in the course of these spiritual transitions, passes through the whole gamut of possible experience —'Nor is there anything/That I have not been.' Yet Yeats is so little anxious to formulate this in poetry that he allows it to lie fallow for thirty-five years before giving it a definitive statement. On first inspection then, it would seem that his magical and occultist persuasions make very little appearance in his verse. There are three poems on Indian themes in *Crossways* (1889), but they are very slight, and Indian in no more than name. The rose symbol that becomes so prominent in his next volume has many values: it is the beloved, it is spiritual beauty, it is the ideal soul of Ireland. It could and doubtless did derive much of its power from the Rosicrucian element in the Golden Dawn. But we do not need to know this; there is nothing in Yeats's use of this symbol that is not recognisable and familiar in the literary tradition. When we come to the love poems of *The Wind Among the Reeds* (CP 99) what is most evident about them is that they *are* love poems—of a highly personal kind, with an odour and a resonance that we have never met before, but still love poems in the long tradition of European love-poetry from Provençe on, celebrating a love that can never be wholly satisfied, could not be what it is if it ever could be wholly satisfied.

Again, poems that can be understood from within the literary tradition. And even at his most wilful and most obscure Yeats in the end always wished to be accessible from the side of the literary tradition, without recourse to his esoteric sources. He was much worried about the possible obscurity of *The Wind Among the Reeds*, the profusion of Irish names and references to Irish myth, either adapted or invented by himself. When the book first appeared it was accompanied by a large body of explanatory notes, often of great beauty and interest in themselves, but so discursive that they do not really make the situation much clearer. In these notes Yeats claims that he had so meditated on the images derived from Irish folklore that 'they had become true symbols'. Now this phrase has a precise meaning in Yeats's terminology; it means that the images have acquired an independent power of

79

their own, that can work without knowledge of their sources or translation into conceptual terms. We are confronted not with a code, but with a self-validating language of feeling. And some enquiry among readers of Yeats who are not professional exegetes or frequenters of university seminars has led me to believe that this is often true, that many readers are content to approach him from this direction and with no seeking for inside knowledge. Without this primary accessibility he would not be the poet he is. But we are not forbidden to enquire further, and Yeats's own constant intellectual vitality is a positive encouragement to do so. An obvious channel is the biographical one. Few readers can have failed to notice that there are two beloveds in *The Wind Among the Reeds*, a proud unreachable beauty by whom the poet is fatally but hopelessly drawn, and a more comforting and available love; and the result is the possession of neither.

> Pale brows, still hands and dim hair,
> I had a beautiful friend
> And dreamed that the old despair
> Would end in love in the end:
> She looked in my heart one day
> And saw your image was there;
> She has gone weeping away. (CP 68)

Not symbols, but persons, who could easily be pursued into Yeats's biography. (Maud Gonne and Olivia Shakespeare, in fact.) But if we look a little more closely we discover that as these poems first appeared in *The Wind Among the Reeds* they were not presented as personal utterances at all. The pieces that in *Collected Poems* are simply attributed to 'the lover', whom we naturally identify with the poet, are distributed among several imagined characters—Aedh, Hanrahan and Michael Robartes. It is Aedh who mourns for the loss of love in the poem just cited; it is Aedh who wishes for the cloths of heaven (CP. 81); it is Hanrahan who laments his restlessness and the loss of quiet (CP 73, 78); it is Michael Robartes who bids his beloved be at peace and remembers forgotten beauty (CP 69). One of Yeats's notes explains that these were all characters in a volume of stories, *The Secret Rose*, that he had brought out two years earlier; but, the note adds, he was using these personages more 'as principles of the mind than as actual personages'. As personages they can be identified from *The Secret Rose*. Aedh is a court poet somewhere in the heroic age, whose severed head goes on singing of his devotion to the Queen after he has been killed in battle. Hanrahan is a lusty vagabond tale-teller, at home by turf fires in cabins. Michael Robertes is an occultist hierophant in fin-de-siècle Dublin, who attempts to lead the narrator into a Golden Dawn initiation, and is killed by orthodox and angry peasants. This removes the poems one stage farther from the realm of private and individual emotion, and a riddling additional note removes them further still. Yeats says that 'only students of the magical tradition' will understand him when he says that Michael Robartes is fire reflected in water, and that Aedh is fire burning by itself. This looks like an attempt to classify the 'principles of the mind' according to the four elements; and indeed it is. It is a reference to

81

the Golden Dawn system of initiation, the first four grades of which are assigned to the four elements, earth air, fire and water; and Yeats's note, which is lengthy, beautiful, alluring, obscure, and a perfect model of how not to write footnotes, goes on to identify these elemental stages with various phases of the imagination —Hanrahan (water), the imagination too volatile to retain a lasting impression; Aedh (fire), the imagination as pure, unchangeable devotion; Michael Robartes (fire reflected in water), the imagination brooding over the greatness and variety of its possessions. Well, we must make what we can of that; or perhaps we are not to make anything of it at all, for in the *Collected Poems*, the form in which almost everyone reads Yeats today, all these annotations, all this rich background material has disappeared; we are left alone with the plain text of the poems.

I have little doubt that this state of innocence is ultimately the desirable one, and that Yeats intended it, by cutting out the anxious hermeneutics of his earlier years. But those of us whose innocence has been irretrievably lost, who have nibbled enough of the fruit of the tree of knowledge to be led inescapably back from the poems themselves to the mind that produced them, can learn something from these convolutions. It is vain to look in Yeats's poems for straightforward transcriptions of his occultist ideas, or even for direct echoes of them. And he is not a poet like Dante or Lucretius whose poetry as a whole expresses a system of philosophy. He has a system, that is continually being worked at and developed, but the relation between the system and the poetry is intricate and indirect. Even the earlier poems, so often thought of as simple and transparent, are not spontaneous *alla prima* sketches; they are built up layer on layer, like paintings of the old masters, the groundwork and the under-painting gleaming darkly through the surface. It is this that accounts for the uncanny power of these apparently frail and slender lyrics; but of course the power is quite independent of any analytical knowledge of how it is generated. Yeats himself was at a loss to explain the poetic function of his occult explorations, but we can detect the outline of an explanation in the notes to *The Wind Among the Reeds*. What appear to be occasional or contingent lyrics, representing the moods and vicissitudes of love are also 'principles of the mind', an attempt at a typology of the imagination. This typology is related to the elements because it is a principle of all hermetic and occultist belief that there is a strict analogy between the microcosm and the macrocosm, the spirit of man and the constitution of the universe. It is this fusion of a free exploration of all the varieties of human experience with a predestined cosmic scheme that gives all Yeats's poetry, from the first to the last, its peculiar density and weight. Much later, at the time of the first version of *A Vision*, he came to realise clearly the object of his occult researches: 'I wished for a system of thought that would leave my imagination free to create as it chose, and yet make all that it created, or could create, part of one history, and that the soul's.' (VA xi)

Anyone who, like Yeats, has become familiar with the Cabalistic Tree of Life, the central complex symbol of the ten Sephiroth or emanations, has already in his

83

possession the outlines of such a system. So we must not be surprised to find that Yeats exercises his imaginative freedom in the widest possible way, without any obvious schematism or obtrusive framework of doctrine, yet does succeed in making all that he creates part of one more-than-personal history. He never uses in poetry any of the esoteric terminology of the Golden Dawn, and the more numinous parts of its symbolism make no appearance. They make a formal principle lying behind the poetry, but are not, direct and untransmuted, the material of which the poetry is made. Yeats had already learnt, as he says in an essay of 1895, 'to discover immortal moods in mortal desires, an undecaying hope in our trivial aspirations, and divine love in sexual passion' (E & I 195). Much of the great poetry of his later life is concerned with personal or public themes, meditations on politics, celebrations of his family and his friends—vigorous, outspoken, confronting with irony or passion the actualities of the daily world. Besides the great meditative sequences in *The Tower* I am thinking of such poems as the 'Introductory Rhymes' to *Responsibilities*, the elegy on Major Robert Gregory, the poem addressed to Parnell's shade and the poems on the 1916 rebellion. The pageant of Yeats's later verse is so abundant and so varied that it is almost absurdly arbitrary to pick out a handful of illustrative moments. It is only possible because Yeats at his greatest is a lyric poet, and it is the essence of lyric poetry that it exists in discrete, individual utterances, each independent and final, whatever its position among its neighbours. It is the glory of lyric poetry to generate moments of intensity and perfection that more extended forms cannot reach. Yeats always retains from his discipleship to Pater a devotion to these moments of greatest intensity. But he had another devotion, only a little less strong—a devotion to the idea of wholeness, of unity of being. What he derived from his endless explorations of unpromising byways of speculation, his elaborate system-building, was the idea of a vast design, so intricate that all experience could find its place within it, and yet be part of the same pattern. We have seen him beginning on this endeavour with the love poems of *The Wind Among the Reeds*. Later he becomes able to situate friends, enemies and indifferent contemporaries in their due position on the Tree of Life so that they can become inhabitants of something more fundamental than an erotic or heroic legend, Yeats often sees Dublin as a city where everything is desperate but nothing serious. 'Easter 1916' celebrates the trans-figuration of Dublin and its inhabitants by the passions of the rebellion, and laments the insufficiency of such passions. But it has a concealed theme; it tacitly celebrates as well the poet's power to see his contem-poraries, tragic, heroic, trivial or debased, as figures in an eternal cosmic drama.

This power is almost unique to Yeats; I can think of no analogue nearer than Dante. Poems like 'Major Robert Gregory', 'The Tower' and 'All Soul's Night' have no parallels in modern poetry. The contemporary characters who are cited by name in Yeats's later poetry form a sort of miniature *Comédie Humaine*; and we remember, perhaps with surprise, Yeats's lifelong admiration for Balzac. It is a total acceptance of experience, including acceptance of all its personal defeats and misdirections:

> I am content to live it all again
> And yet again, if it be life to pitch
> Into the frog-spawn of a blind man's ditch,
> A blind man battering blind men . . .
>
> I am content to follow to follow to its source
> Every event in action or in thought;
> Measure the lot; forgive myself the lot!
> When such as I cast out remorse
> So great a sweetness flows into the breast
> We must laugh and we must sing,
> We are blest by everything,
> Everything we look upon is blest.   (CP 267)

But this is an acceptance of experience so total that it ends by transcending itself and taking the spirit out of experience altogether. On occasion Yeats can bear witness to that too, as in these lines on Florence Emery, once an actress and a famous beauty, who had left the world and died in a distant country.

> Before that end much had she ravelled out
> From a discourse in figurative speech
> By some learned Indian
> On the soul's journey, how it is whirled about,
> Wherever the orbit of the moon can reach,
> Until it plunge into the sun;
> And there, free and yet fast,

Magic and Poetry

Being both Chance and Choice,
Forget its broken toys
And sink into its own delight at last.   (CP 258)

Theologically and morally this dialectic in Yeats never reaches a resolution. But there is another kind of resolution, which has not perhaps been recognised as it deserves. We find it in the many-sided vision of the later poetry, able to encompass so much of the varied and the contingent, while at the same time transmuting it into the perennial and the archetypal. This is an achievement not possible for the pure lyric poet without, to use Yeats's words, a system of thought that would make all part of one history. And I have found a comprehension of this in a place where it would hardly have been expected. Earlier on I cited an instance of blank failure in response to Yeats's speculative activities —the surprisingly crass remarks of Auden. It is agreeable to end with a contrary example—an example of immediate, intuitive understanding.

On 8 November 1930 Virginia Woolf met Yeats at a party of Lady Ottoline Morrell's, and the record of this encounter in her diary is an act of homage and respect not very common in the annals of Bloomsbury.[3] Though not unused to distinguished company, she was clearly somewhat overwhelmed, both by his presence and his discourse. She describes him as 'vital and supple, highly charged and altogether seasoned and generous'. And what is most striking about her reaction is that although she knows nothing of Yeats's thought, and it would seem not very much of his poetry, she has the sense of a large background of ideas and speculations that give weight and form to all he says. He talks of dreams and various states of the soul: 'So familiar was he' she writes 'that I perceived that he had worked out a complete psychology that I could only catch on to momentarily, in my alarming ignorance.' He goes on to modern poetry and its deficiencies; they are inevitable 'because we are at the end of an era. Here was another system of thought, of which I could only catch fragments.' And she concludes, in a tone that contrasts markedly with the confident ideological assurance with which she was normally surrounded—'but how crude and jaunty my own theories were beside his: indeed I got a tremendous sense of the intricacy of his art; also of its meaning, its seriousness, its importance, which wholly engrosses this large active minded immensely vitalised man.'

IV. *A Vision:* Queries and Reflections

1. Virginia Woolf, on a short and far from intimate encounter with Yeats, realised at once that he was in possession of a complete system of thought, of which she could only catch fragments. She was impelled to an act of homage that points without knowing it in the direction we should take if we are seeking the warrant and the validation of Yeats's occult researches. The largeness and integrity of the creative personality that resulted from them is their manifest justification; and I think this is felt by all serious readers of Yeats, whether they have cared to follow his explorations or not. But this still leaves many questions unanswered, and a certain kind of mind unsatisfied—not necessarily the 'levelling rancorous rational sort of mind' that Yeats deplored. Even the congenial reader of *A Vision* may decently ask how Yeats intended us to take it. And whether we can take it as he intended; and if not what we are to do with it.

2. To begin at the end we understand most easily; we

know the literary kind to which *A Vision* belongs. It is an apocalypse, a revelation, of which there are numerous examples in our culture and neighbouring ones. Revelations come in various ways: they are brought by angels; the heavens open and visions are seen; dictation is received from unseen powers. In Yeats's case the revelation came through the medium-ship of his wife. This is a more domestic and familiar line of communication, without the transcendental authority of many of the classic revelations of the past. The 'communicators', as Yeats generally called them, are unknown and unidentified. They are imperious but not infallible. They do not claim to be speaking with divine authorisation. Yeats can question their status and at times argue with their conclusions.

He is quite clear about this. 'Much that has happened, much that has been said, suggests that the communicators are the personalities of a dream shared by my wife, by myself, occasionally by others.' (VB 22) The others include occasionally the dead. Yeats affirms categorically his belief in the communion of the living and the dead, and those who want to quarrel with his premisses can begin here. But he goes on to say that the dead are fantastic and deceitful, and quotes an Orphic warning—'The Gates of Pluto must not be unlocked, within is a people of dreams.'

Yeats opens himself freely to his vision, but there is always a substratum of scepticism and reserve.

3. Asked whether he believed in the actual existence of his 'circuits of the sun and moon', i.e. his psychological and historical symbolism of phases, circles, cones and

gyres, he replied 'If, sometimes, overwhelmed by miracle as all men must be when in the midst of it, I have taken such periods literally, my reason has soon recovered: and now that the system stands clear in my imagination I regard them as stylistic arrangements of experience.' (VB 25)

To those who are repelled by the arbitrary and baffling nature of his symbolism (and that must include most readers of *A Vision*) his answer is simply that this is the way such things come; and he appeals to widespread precedents, citing some of the classic examples of obscure and fantastic imagery used as the vehicle of cosmic insights. 'One remembers the six wings of Daniel's angels, the Pythagorean numbers, a venerated book of the Cabala where the beard of God winds in and out among the stars, its hairs all numbered, those complicated mathematical tables that Kelly saw in Dr Dee's black scrying stone.' (VB 23)

Thus Yeats claims the kinship of his vision with the prophetic and visionary literature of the past.

4. It would be foolish to ask why Yeats chose this mode of expression. He did not choose. The matter of *A Vision* came as it came, not to be resisted, and so very largely did the form. But we can well ask why a construction so forbidding and so bizarre should be so passionately welcomed by Yeats, what he hoped it would achieve. He was quite aware of the decorum of consecutive reasoning, even though he did not follow it. He knew that he was proclaiming conclusions that often fell within the domain of the philosophers, though reached by methods that philosophers could

not sanction or acknowledge, and he was always glad to find philosophical support where he could. But he believed too that modern philosophy had no words of power, that even if it were to prove by logic a transcendental truth it would leave the imagination subject to nature as before. 'The great books . . . beget new books, whole generations of books, but life goes on unchanged. It was not so with ancient philosophy, for the ancient philosopher had something to reinforce his thought—the Gods, the Sacred Dead, Egyptian Theurgy, the Priestess Diotima.' (VA 251) Yeats is going back here to the world of the Neoplatonists, from whom much of his occult tradition derives. And this is a world where philosophy is impregnated (or contaminated, as the modern philosopher would say) with a teeming mythic and imaginative life. The ancient philosopher 'could assume, perhaps even prove, that every condition of mind discovered by analysis, even that which is timeless, spaceless, is present vivid experience to some being, and that we could in some degree communicate with this being while still alive, and after our death share in the experience.' (VA 252)

It is Yeats's belief that some glimpse of this assurance of a supersensible world and the possibility of communion with it is part of the human heritage, never entirely lost, and it is to recapture this linkage that he records the experience of *A Vision*, in the baffling, logic-defeating manner in which such experiences have been recorded from the beginning of history. He says so, in the last sentence of the first version of the book: 'That we may believe that all men possess the supernatural faculties I would restore to the philosopher his mythology' (VA 252).

Those who want to quarrel with Yeats's purpose can begin here, and probably might as well end here too.

5. O blessed word mythology, which through the centuries has covered such a multitude of sins, from the unexemplary amours of Zeus to the bogus mathematics of Levi-Strauss, which even to those who use it in the most honorific sense remains an ill-defined entity of uncertain standing. Mythology can be the vehicle of religious truth, or what claims to be so, but itself it is something less than religion—less exigent, less assuming. Mythology can deal with the creation, with the consummation of the world, and with everything that lies between; but its presentations are rarely definitive or final. Most myths exist in alternative versions, or have rival interpretations, and there is tolerance between them. 'Some suppose. . . .', 'as others report' —such phrases abound in the dictionaries of mythology. But not in the Athanasian creed.

The significance of a myth cannot be encapsulated in a formula. Yeats is indeed partly concerned with doctrine, a doctrine about a spiritual world which could have been expressed in doctrinal or credal terms. But when he talks of restoring to the philosopher his mythology he is thinking of another kind of expression; a myth may be embodied in a fable, an image, a diagram or a dance. I take it that Yeats's 'mythology' is equivalent to his 'stylistic arrangement of experience'. Most of the statements of purpose in *A Vision* carefully avoid literal commitment.

When Yeats offered to spend the rest of his life in developing the philosophy of the unknown communicators they forbade it, saying 'we come to give you metaphors for poetry.' This throws out a lifeline to hard-pressed commentators, and could have been used as an escape-route by Yeats himself: metaphors for poetry—valid for the nonce, within the framework of the poem, with no status outside it. But he does not take this course either. His metaphors are formed into a system, though not into a chain of reasoning. He has a great deal of the Keatsian Negative Capability—'when a man is capable of being in uncertainties, mysteries, doubts, without any irritable reaching after fact and reason'; but this rests always on a substratum of conviction.

6. It is of course possible to come bustling up with a straight question and demand a straight answer—as is done by Harold Bloom, in a mood of unwonted positivism. 'What precisely is Yeats trying to say about human life, and has he found an adequate image for his insight, if it is one?'[1] But if this question could be answered in the terms in which it is put it would not have been necessary to write *A Vision* at all.

It had been an article of Yeats's belief from his earliest days that the Great Memory, 'the mind of Nature herself', the *Anima Mundi* could be evoked by symbols. Symbols meant something quite positive and definite—verbal formulae, and ceremonial, but also coloured shapes, talismans and hieroglyphs, and sometimes natural objects. It is axiomatic that their effect is not a function of meaning or intellectual content. They

work by other agencies. Yeats found nothing repug-
nant in the 'barbarous words' of evocation that he read
about in Iamblichus, and takes satisfaction in symbols
so old that their meaning has been forgotten. No doubt
he often made the most of this way of thinking, *pour
épater*; but there is no doubt either that he had a
perfectly serious and, as he thought, well-founded
conviction of the power of non-discursive symbolism,
of imagery that cannot be translated into intellectual
terms, or only partially and imperfectly. *A Vision* is a
complex assembly of such images, and the central
portion of it relies largely on a non-verbal symbol for
its effect. So the answer to Bloom's question is that
there is no answer, in terms that would satisfy him. If
we are to put this work to the question it must be in
another way.

7. It should be said at once that much of the symbolism
of *A Vision* is extremely disconcerting. Untranslatable
non-discursive symbolism derives much of its efficacy
from neighbourhood—from kinship and assimilation
to one of the great fountains of public imagery, such as
the Apocalypse of St John, the classical pantheon, the
movements of the starry heavens—still relatively
familiar even today. Over large tracts of *A Vision* Yeats
denies himself this source of strength and intelligibility.
Whether his alien apparatus was devised by himself or
received ready-made from his mentors has never been
clear. But what I believe is clear is that some of it works
and some does not.

What does work, fortunately, is the largest and most
crucial part of the system—the Great Wheel and the

long detailed description of the phases (VB Book I); the analysis of the historical cycles in 'Dove or Swan' (VB, Book V); and the description of the after-life in 'The Soul in Judgment' (VB Book III). We return to these in a moment; but first to filter out the dross. The detailed psychology—the four faculties and the relation between them (VB80–92,96–9) is important to the scheme, is ingeniously devised, and has some flashes of brilliance, but in general it brings less illumination than it should. The ancillary elaborations of this (VB 92–5, 100–104) —the four principles, perfections, automatisms, etc— are hopelessly fussy and superfluous, but easily dispensable as they are quite unintegrated with the main structure. The worst confusion, a source of endless exasperation and dismay, is unhappily in one of the best-known places, since its vocabulary penetrates into some of the famous later poetry. It is the machinery of the two interpenetrating cone-shaped gyres by which Yeats tries to illustrate the enantiodromia at the heart of his system. (VB 187–215; 67–80) Happily, the Great Wheel itself provides a far more lucid alternative illustration of the same phenomena. Finally, it is wise to pass lightly and selectively over the section on the Great Year of the Ancients (VB 243–63) and go straight on to its more lucid historical entailments in 'Dove or Swan'.

These dismissals are fairly extensive (about eighty pages), possibly mistaken, and quite likely impertinent. I risk them because I feel strongly that if the more cluttered and ill-arranged apartments are simply shut off the chances of a satisfactory progress through the rest of the edifice are greatly increased.

A Vision: *Queries and Reflections*

8. Then there is the question of the two versions. But that need not detain us long. Yeats expressly repudiates the first, 1925, version (VA), except for the parts he repeats in the second version of 1937 (VB). 'The first version of this book, *A Vision*, except the section on the twenty-eight phases, and that called "Dove or Swan" which I repeat without change, fills me with shame. I had misinterpreted the geometry and in my ignorance of philosophy failed to understand distinctions on which the coherence of the whole depended.' (VB 19)

The two sections repeated, the twenty-eight phases and 'Dove or Swan' are substantial and of central importance. In fact Yeats repeats rather more than he says; the two poems 'The Phases of the Moon' and 'All Soul's Night' are also reproduced, and the Table of the Faculties. In all, 130 pages out of the 250 pages of *Vision* A reappear unaltered in *Vision* B, and the 30-page section 'The Gates of Pluto' from A is more or less paraphrased and rearranged as 'The Soul in Judgment' in B. The prefatory and fictional material of A is abandoned and replaced by new prefaces and fictions, but these are not material to the system. What Yeats was dissatisfied with and amends considerably in B is the geometrical material of cones and gyres, and that connected with the Great Year. Whether the B version improves matters much remains doubtful. There are definitions and isolated *aperçus* in A that we should be unwilling to lose; but the general upshot is that everything of substance in A is either reproduced identically in B or is present in an amended form. And since B has also the unfictionalised Introduction (VB 8–25) recounting the circumstances of composition, there can be no doubt that it should be accepted as the definitive text, though it may be supplemented with passages from A when they are helpful.

9. The principal symbol is the Great Wheel. It is the key to all the rest, but I think there is a tendency to expect too much of it. Because it vaguely recalls the spheres and circles in Platonic myth, because it suggests dim analogies with Ptolemaic astronomy, which Yeats actually makes use of in Book II, and because Yeats in the past had always been so ready with astrological imagery it is easy to think of the Wheel as the outline of a cosmology. But it is not. It has nothing to do with the starry heavens. The phases of the moon are only a convenience of notation, and the half-hearted attempt to introduce a solar symbolism as well (dark of the moon = full sun) never comes to anything (see VB 82,196) and is virtually abandoned.

The Wheel is primarily a classification of psychological types, but it is always more than that, for it is immediately fused with the doctrine (found in Theosophy and in certain Gnostic sects) that it is the destiny of man to pass through all these possibilities of experience in successive incarnations. The wheel symbol is traditional and widespread among reincarnationists, found also among the Pythagoreans and in Indian thought—though it should be noted that Yeats uses it in a different and more elaborate way.

The Wheel with its twenty-eight phases represents the twenty-eight incarnations which fulfil the whole possible range of human experience; and this pattern is so fundamental that it appears, on a larger or smaller scale, in every aspect of human life. Man passes through the same phases in a single incarnation, in a single judgment or act of thought—though many of these movements must be imperceptible. Since the Wheel is 'every completed movement of thought or life' it also realises itself in collective life, in the progression of cultures; it is the rhythm of history. But comprehensive as this pattern is, it is confined to human experience. There is no transition to the macrocosm, as in the more grandiose occultist schemes, or indeed in Dante, where moral experience becomes the pattern for the structure of the universe. Yeats may have been willing to make this claim, but he does not do so in *A Vision*.

10. The driving principle of Yeats's thought is the interaction of opposites. In his youth he found it in Blake—'without contraries is no progression'; and it is prominent in *Per Amica*, the work that immediately preceded *A Vision* and already contains the embryo of its central ideas.

The lunar symbolism is a happy equivalent for this, with its arresting contrast between the dark, when the moon is 'hid in her vacant interlunar cave', and the brilliant effulgence of the moon at the full. And in between are twenty-six phases, waxing and waning, familiar, beautiful, visible every month if we care to look. But there are no astrological claims—that the phases of the moon cause or dictate the development of man's nature; it is an appropriate metaphor, no more. And it is not primarily a verbal metaphor; indeed the attempt to describe it in words soon becomes clumsy, while the diagram on p.81 of VB is simple and lucid.

The use of the phases of the moon as a notation means of course a quite arbitrary division of the psychological types into twenty-eight. If Yeats or his teachers had chosen a clock-face as a pattern, they would have been twelve. This might have been better. One often feels in reading the descriptions of the twenty-eight types that the divisions have been cut too fine and the distinctions are consequently not clear, even though the general progress and direction is not in doubt.

11. The two poles of Yeats's antithesis are not like anything in Christian philosophy. They are given no moral evaluation, they are not good and evil. The light and the dark, the full moon and the moon occulted, are like the Yang and the Yin of Chinese philosophy, though without the sexual connotation. Yeats has various terms for describing this opposition, and they are evaluatively quite neutral. The dark of the moon (phase 1) is *primary*, and the full moon (phase 15) is *antithetical*. These are further clarified as *objective* and *subjective*. It soon becomes apparent that Yeats's sympathies lie with the antithetical/subjective, and that he sees the primary/objective as inferior. But this is his artist's preference. As parts of the system they are co-ordinate and equal powers.

Further elucidations of this fundamental polarity come scattered throughout *A Vision*. The antithetical is that which creates, the primary that which serves. In antithetical phases man struggles with himself, in primary phases he struggles with the world. As the antithetical phases approach their climax at phase 15 there is a continual growth in beauty; as the primary phases return towards phase 1 they grow progressively more deformed.

This is one of the cases where Yeats's concepts are not adequately defined by the labels he gives them, and do not coincide exactly with any that we are familiar with in other places; but in reading *A Vision* and the later work generally we find ourselves becoming accustomed to them and recognise their nature without any necessary recourse to a formal definition.

12. The phases are numbered and a particular man is classified from the position of Will, this being the dominant and identifying faculty. But it is only one of four which go to make up the human psyche—Will, Mask, Creative Mind and Body of Fate. I follow Vendler here[2] in preferring the definitions given in VA (14,15) because they are clearer; but even so I partly resort to paraphrase.

Will is 'the bias by which the soul is classified and its phase fixed'; it is the soul's intrinsic tone of feeling, prior to all desire, aspiration or action.

Mask is correlative to Will; it is 'the image of what we wish to become', the object of aspiration and desire.

Creative Mind means 'intellect, as intellect was understood before the close of the seventeenth century —all the mind that is consciously constructive.'

Body of Fate is 'the physical and mental environment', which stands opposite to the creative intellect.

The reader's initial response is I think to refuse this strange classification, and try to assimilate it to a more

101

familiar quaternity: the Jungian one, perhaps—
Thought, Feeling, Intuition and Sensation. But they do
not fit; nor do any of the other quaternities that bedeck
occultist thought—the elements, the compass-points,
the Evangelists or Ezekiel's fourfold cherubim. The
Blakean, Shelleyan and Freudian parallels suggested
by Bloom are ridiculous.[3] Again we find that Yeats's
concepts do not exactly correspond to any that we
recognise; but again, on increased familiarity they
become more distinct. Mask as the object of aspiration
and desire is always at opposite phase to Will. Body of
Fate, as the brute fact which intellect has to contend
with, is always at opposite phase to Creative Mind. The
relation between these two pairs is less clear.

13. Up to now it has been possible to regard Yeats's
symbolism as being in the service of his psychology.
Whether or not we are willing to see them as successive
incarnations, the twenty-eight phases and their return
journey between the objective and subjective poles make
up an intelligible diagram of human potentialities, a
taxonomy of psychological types, which in some measure
we can match with our experience, as we are invited to
do by the biographical examples. The four faculties
divided into two pairs, will and its object, thought and
its object, with their complementary interactions, also
make an intelligible diagram of the internal dynamics
of the psyche. On this basis we could give a sort of
answer to Bloom's question 'What is Yeats trying to
say about human life?' Yeats is trying to say that the
nature of any individual life depends upon its direction
(is it moving towards self-realisation at phase 15, or

towards submission to the Other at phase 1?); and upon how far it has travelled between these two poles. Its internal state at any given time depends on the ever-changing tension between will and its object, thought and its object. When the circle is complete it begins again; when the tension between the Faculties reaches its climax the movement reverses itself and begins to go the other way. It is a psychology of dynamism, of opposing tensions, offering no state of rest. That is to say something about human life. The symbolism, though difficult to grasp at first, is not more difficult than the ideas behind it, and has the extra supererogatory imaginative power that a symbol must have if it is not to be a mere useless riddle.

14. But beyond this stage (I mean this stage of the argument; we cannot pinpoint it exactly in the text, for there is much repetition and ellipsis) we encounter two difficulties of a much more serious kind. The first is a good deal of muddle and faulty exposition. The second is an uneasy sense that the symbolism is taking over, acquiring a life of its own, no longer in any intelligible relation to the human realities it is supposed to elucidate.

The muddles have mostly been mentioned already. First come the superfluous and dangling categories which are not afterwards made use of—perfections, automatisms, discords, contrasts etc. These, as we have suggested, can easily be dispensed with. Then there is the daunting solid geometry, cones and gyres. This can be left to those whose imagination can compass it. (Mine cannot) Nothing essential is lost without it. A gnomic but expressive passage on p.73 says most of what matters:

> The *Faculties* can be represented as two opposing cones so drawn that the *Will* of one is the *Mask* of the other, the *Creative Mind* of the one the *Body of Fate* of the other. Everything that wills can be desired, resisted or accepted, every creative act can be seen as fact, every *Faculty* is alternately shield and sword.

15. The growing independence, waywardness and complication of the symbolism is more formidable. (This section will be intolerable to all except aficionados.)

The Table of the Four Faculties (VB 96–9) is essential but confusing. It sets out in tabular form the title or short description or each Faculty as it arises in every phase. Mask and Creative Mind have true and false forms.

For example, Phase 3. *Will*: Beginning of ambition. *Mask*: True, Simplification through intensity; False, Dispersal. *Creative Mind*: True, Supersensual Receptivity, False, Pride. *Body of Fate*: Enforced love of another.

This is confusing because it does *not* represent the psychic condition of a man whose Will is at phase 3. For that we have to turn to phase 3 in the detailed description of the twenty-eight incarnations. Here we find that when Will is at phase 3 Mask is at its opposite, phase 17; Creative Mind is somewhere else again, actually phase 27; and Body of Fate at its opposite, phase 13.

And so with all the other phases. The oppositions are easily seen by consulting the diagram, the positions of the Faculties by consulting the detailed descriptions of the Incarnations.

So-called rules are given (VB 91–2) for finding true and false Masks, true and false Creative Mind and Body of Fate. But they are not rules, and they are quite unintelligible.

However, there *are* rules, given the position of Will, that enable us to find Mask, Creative Mind and Body of Fate, though Yeats does not give them. They are as follows:

Will moves counter-clockwise round the Wheel, starting from phase 1.

Mask moves counter-clockwise, starting from phase 15.

Creative Mind moves clockwise, starting from phase 1.

Body of Fate moves clockwise, starting from phase 15.

By applying these rules the state of the Faculties for any phase can be found, and it will be found to agree both with what is given in the description of the twenty-eight Incarnations and in the Table of the Faculties.

For example, *Will* at phase 7 (6 places counter-clockwise from 1).

Mask at its opposite (6 places counter-clockwise from 15) phase 21.

Creative Mind (6 places clockwise from 1) phase 23.

Body of Fate at its opposite (6 places clockwise from 15) phase 9.

It is all quite systematic, but since these rules are nowhere clearly given in the text (though obscurely mentioned at VB 74 and 80) the system is not easy to perceive, and I confess it was years before I saw what was going on. Others have doubtless been more acute; but I give the rules here for the benefit of those as imperceptive as myself.

16. What we have here is an elaborate ballet of the Faculties, one pair moving in one direction, the other in the opposite direction; and the individual members of each pair starting from opposite points.

This has a symmetry of motion that I suppose gives a certain aesthetic satisfaction. But can anyone believe for a moment that this elaborate schematism has anything to do with the constitution of the human mind? The twenty-eight phases are a possible description of the types of human motivation, the four faculties a possible description of the forces at work within the psyche; and they seem to have been devised with some reference to experience. But the dance of the four faculties and the rules for their mutual relation is schematism for its own sake; it has no reference whatever to anything encountered in life or deducible from it. From the way this part of the doctrine is presented—dogmatic, unargued, unpersuasive—we might surmise that most of it came from the unknown instructors, and that Yeats simply took it as it came.

But we do not know about this; and we do not know because those who are in a position to know—i.e. those who have been allowed to inspect the original documents—conspicuously refrain from telling us.

Yeats's own comments however reveal that there was certainly much working up of the original material. The point to note here is a teasing discrepancy between what looks like descriptive psychology and what looks like *a priori* system-building. Any formula for the dynamics of the psyche—Freud's Id, Ego and Superego, Jung's four faculties, the Platonic threefold classification—must be more or less mythological; but most of them fulfil some evident analytical or moral purpose. Part of the Yeatsian scheme does so too; the subjective/objective antithesis, the one diminishing as the other increases, seems rationally satisfying and makes some sort of empirical sense. But the rest of the scheme—the sustained and rigorous opposition between Will and Mask, Creative Mind and Body of Fate, the counter-clockwise movement of the first pair, the clockwise movement of the second—seems to fulfil only the demands of a geometrical pattern. And since the mysterious affinity of geometry with the motions of the human soul is no longer part of our intellectual experience, it runs the risk of looking ingenious but meaningless.

17. Nevertheless, two reminders seem to be in order. The first is that arithmetical and geometrical patterning of this kind, and the application of it to the dynamics of the soul, to morality and religion, is a very ancient human activity. It goes back to Pythagoras, and passes from him to Plato. Bertrand Russell remarks on the profound influence of geometry and mathematics on philosophy and theology, and goes so far as to say that theology in its exact scholastic form takes its style from

Euclid.[4] Yeats is following in the same tradition, and indeed is aware of it, as he shows by citing among the precursors of *A Vision* the numbers of Pythagoras, Dr Dee's mathematical tables and the diagrams in Law's *Boehme*. A passage in *On the Boiler* commends 'those Greek proportions that carry into plastic art the Pythagorean numbers, those faces which are divine because all there is empty and measured.' And the late poem 'The Statues' revolves around the same theme. I have to confess that I can make little of this way of thinking, but it is quite clear that it has been found significant by men of subtle mind at various times in the past.

The second point we need to remember is Yeats's long-standing attitude to 'symbols'. Symbols, it will be recalled, need not be verbal or discursive. They can be visual, geometric, numerical. And they can have an intrinsic power. A talismanic image can have a meaning, though a meaning that has never been put into words; and it can affect the mind, though its meaning has never reached the level of conscious awareness.

The Wheel and its internal movements is such a talisman, and a very rich one. The principles of its movement are quite simple, but the resultant pattern (the twenty-eight phases and their mutual relations) is intricate. And Yeats feels this as a powerful symbolic design. How many of his readers today are capable of doing so is another question. One answer I think is that everyone finds brilliant flashes, occasional tantalising glimpses from inside the Wheel to a fragment of the outer world. The description of phase 24 with its examples (Queen Victoria, Galsworthy and Lady Gregory) is a case in point. But some of the other phases remain quite opaque, or lead to mere bewilderment. And we ought probably to understand that the efficacy of the Wheel as a symbol is not really to be judged in this way at all. If it is 'empty and measured' rather than obviously related to life, that for Yeats is part of its virtue. Or, a more reassuring way of looking at it, we can see it as something like an orrery or planetarium—a working model, illustrating in a small-scale, more or less graspable form, much larger motions not visible to the naked eye, yet of fundamental importance to the life that it seems to pass by.

18. The part of *A Vision* that we have been considering (all in VB, Book I) is central, and can with justice be called a system. Whatever its descriptive value, it is self-contained, consistent, and is thus rationally comprehensible. It is evidently however part of a larger and looser system, including the historical scheme, which applies the principles of the Wheel to nations and cultures (Book V), and the account of the progress of the soul between incarnations (Book III), which is an insertion, consistent and connected with the rest but partly derived from other sources. These are substantial, easily reconciled with the central argument, and need cause no difficulty. There is however a penumbra of images in Book I Part II and in Book II, some of them partly worked up into systematic form, some left merely miscellaneous. It has already been suggested that these appendages are better abandoned, and comprehension is made much easier if the Four

Principles (VB 187 ff.) are allowed to go with them. I feel some compunction in relegating the Principles in this way; they have enchanting names—Husk, Passionate Body, Spirit and Celestial Body—and they clearly meant something to Yeats; but try as I will I cannot fit them into the system or see them as anything but shadows or echoes of the Faculties. Yeats tells us that he knew nothing of the Principles when he wrote VA—'a script had been lost through frustration or my own carelessness'. This intrusion of sublunary accident arouses the suspicion in my mind that the Principles are indeed mere doublets, mistaken or alternative reformulations of the Faculties. And pending further illumination I must leave it at that.

There are however two of these supernumerary symbols which float continually through both versions of *A Vision*, have no easily comprehensible place in the total scheme, yet recur often enough to carry a good deal of weight and to demand separate consideration. They are the Daimon and the Thirteenth Cone.

19. The Daimon is an elusive concept, for it seems from time to time to change its nature, function, and even its sex. Yeats was of course familiar with the daimons of Neoplatonism, who were non-human spirits or minor deities, and have their later equivalents among the fairies and elementals that populate the lower part of the occult world. The term occurs in its commoner and more pejorative spelling in Yeats's Golden Dawn motto, *Demon est deus inversus*; though what was meant by it has never become quite clear. He first uses the term in his own special sense in *Per Amica*

Silentia Lunae, and it thereafter becomes prominent in VA, rather less so in VB.

In *Per Amica Silentia Lunae* there is a long development of the doctrine of the anti-self, and it is here that the Daimon makes his appearance. The doctrine, most memorably expressed in the poem 'Ego Dominus Tuus', is the germ of the antinomies and oppositions that become so important in *A Vision*. It is the idea that the truly creative man does not seek to 'find himself', but to find all that is not himself, his own opposite, and in this opposition to find the fullness of power. Yeats first calls the opposite the Mask; but later personifies it as the Daimon. 'The Daimon comes not as like to like but seeking its own opposite, for man and Daimon feed the hunger in one another's hearts.' A riddling note distinguishes between the permanent and the impermanent Daimon, the latter being an occasional visitant to a seance, as Leo Africanus appeared to be at first, the former, the permanent Daimon, being an enduring psychic companion, a sort of antithetical guardian angel, as Leo Africanus later for a time claimed to be. In either case the Daimon is a separate and independent spirit, and may be either non-human or the spirit of an 'illustrious dead man'. Nations, cultures, schools of thought too have their tutelary daimons, again opposite in nature to themselves. (VB 209)

VA continues much of the speculation of *Per Amica Silentia Lunae*, but with decided turns of its own; and the Daimon here seems to have become a part of man's mind rather than an independent existent—the part of man's mind that is normally in the dark. 'But there is another mind or another part of our mind in this

111

darkness, that is yet to its own perception in the light.' (VA 27) The Daimon is here referred to as 'she', being always of the opposite sex to man. She is in fact the Jungian Anima—a contra-sexual image, the interpreter and representative of the unconscious as a whole, always opposite to the Will or consciousness of man; a main agent in what Jung calls the integration of the personality, and Yeats calls Unity of Being. Yeats's thought often approximates to Jung's; here it seems to be following an identical path. A lyrical passage at VA 228 describes the Daimon in terms that recall both the Anima, as she appears in the Jungian integration dreams, and the Monna Lisa of Pater, also a symbol of total experience. But the outline of the Daimon remains wavering. Sometimes it stands for what the man lacks, his opposite; sometimes for the new totality that is created by the union of the opposites—what Jung calls the Self, the man re-centred and transformed. In VB 83 the Daimon is referred to as 'the ultimate self' of the man. So we remain uncertain whether the Daimon is the whole or a complementary part. Uncertain too whether it is an independent spirit or a component of man's psychic totality. Perhaps in view of Yeats's belief that the borders of our minds are ever shifting, and certain speculations of his about group souls, these possibilities are not mutually exclusive. At VB 189–90 the Daimon seems to have lost its feminine character, and appears again to be a separate spirit, with will, desires and 'hungers' of its own, and it seeks union with other daimons as well as with men. And at VB 239 the Daimon is expressly differentiated from 'some ordinary discarnate spirit'.

So descriptions of the Daimon hover indeterminately between the psychology of Book I and the pneumatology of Book III. I think we can see a reason for this. The Daimon is a first tentative embodiment of the principle of antinomy, antithesis, opposition, contariety, that was to be so elaborately systematised in *A Vision*. As a relic of an earlier formulation it cannot properly be fitted into the system, yet it is too vivid and imaginatively living to be abandoned. It is nearer perhaps to 'a metaphor for poetry' than most other elements of *A Vision*. The obscurity of its status is confirmed when we learn—as we do in several places—that its natural habitat is that mysterious region the Thirteenth Cone.

20. The Thirteenth Cone, also called the Thirteenth Cycle, or Gyre, or Sphere, presents a knottier problem than the Daimon. At least we know of the Daimon that it is a spirit, possibly a once-human spirit, attached by some affinity-in-opposition to a living man. And it appears as part of a well-developed and wide-ranging Yeatsian doctrine. But the Thirteenth Cone is announced out of the blue, unrelated, a name and no more, and we are at a loss to know whether it is a locality, a historical period, an undifferentiated slice of time, a state of affairs or a supernatural force. The nomenclature need not cause much difficulty. Cone, Gyre and Cycle all mean the same thing—a complete revolution of the Wheel, the full circle of twenty-eight incarnations. But Yeats several times calls it the Thirteenth Sphere, and he explains that it is really a sphere, 'a phaseless sphere', but can only be perceived by men as a cone (VB

193). The geometry of this is impenetrable, but a meaning can I think be divined. A complete cycle of twenty-eight incarnations is ultimately a totality, in which antinomies and separable phases are totally submerged; and this is aptly symbolised by a sphere, without parts or divisions. But man involved in the cycle can only see the movement as antinomy—the light cone widening to a circle, the dark cone narrowing to a point. But this seems equally true of all cycles; why it should be mentioned particularly in connection with the Thirteenth is not clear.

And why the *Thirteenth* Cone anyway? It seems to imply that we already know about the other twelve. No explanation is given in VA; we hear little of the Thirteenth Cone—only that it is the abode of certain spirits, including all Daimons. An explanation begins to appear at VB 202. A Great Wheel of twenty-eight incarnations is considered to take some two thousand odd years. Twelve such Wheels (Cones, Cycles or Gyres) make up a Great Year, identified with the Great Year of ancient astronomy in which the precession of the Equinox is completed. Nothing is said here about a Thirteenth Cycle, but if we turn back to VB 193 we find that there is such an entity, and that it has a very lofty status—it is the locus of ultimate reality. 'The ultimate reality because neither one nor many, concord nor discord, is symbolised as a phaseless sphere, but as all things fall into a series of antinomies in human experience it becomes the moment it is thought of what I shall presently describe as the Thirteenth Cone.'

This is very puzzling. The first twelve cones or cycles are ordinary temporal periods, defined as being of about two thousand years each. If the Thirteenth Cycle is of the same kind as the others, as its name implies, it must be a sort of intercalary period between two Great Years. But this makes nonsense of the astronomy. The precession of the equinox cannot be supposed to stand still for two thousand years to provide Yeats's mentors with a resounding metaphor. Indeed the two thousand years for a complete cycle of twenty-eight incarnations is already at odds with Yeats's own system. It only allows seventy years for each incarnation—enough for the space of a lifetime, but leaving no room for the long periods between lives, so elaborately analysed in Book III. In other parts of the present argument there seem to be other confusions. There is an apparent mix-up at VB 202 about whether the Great Year is of twelve or thirteen cycles (unless we are to believe that twice twelve is twenty-six); and there is a curious indifference to whether its length is 26,000 or 36,000 years. At VB 210 there is an attempt to explain the relation of the Thirteenth cone to the other cones which only makes confusion worse confounded. I assume therefore that it is no use trying to make sense of the astronomical/numerical argument of this part of VB (Book II), and that the explanation of the Thirteenth Cone must be sought on other lines.

21. Turning again to VB 193 we can plausibly see that the Thirteenth Cone is not an additional member to a temporal series, but is something outside time altogether. 'All things are present as an eternal instant' to spirits when they inhabit that sphere. But they are not so visible to creatures still bound to time, and

Yeats's instructors therefore put forward instead the idea of an eternal Record, 'where the images of all past events remain for ever'. This is the concept familiar in occultist literature of 'the pictures in the astral light', Madame Blavatsky's Akashic records, what Yeats had earlier called the Great Memory, and Blake 'the bright sculptures of Los's hall'. Looked at in this way the Thirteenth Cone seems to be a timeless realm, offering a haven from the endless inexorable revolution of the Yeatsian wheels. As such it would fulfil a want which many of Yeats's readers have felt. But it is not successfully integrated into the system, and it remains curiously unanchored to the history and psychology of which it ought to be the completion.

The Thirteenth Cone is in some way the agent of freedom; it turns into a phaseless sphere when 'the time has come for our deliverance. . . . Within it live all souls that have been set free' (VB 210). It is called by every man his freedom, and it is also something that is *in* every man. These enigmatic pronouncements are not easy to reconcile; the Thirteenth Cone seems at the same time to be a region, a period of time and a component of the human psyche. And as an accommodation to the weakness of human understanding it can be conceived as a Record where all the past is simultaneously co-existent—a concept that has little obvious connection with freedom.

If the Daimon is a first imagining of something that was more fully developed later, the Thirteenth Cone is an unfinished attempt at something that was never fully developed. Adverse critics of Yeats have described his system as a complete determinism. This has been

116

convincingly answered by Ellmann: 'It does not work that way at all. Man may choose between several alternatives, such as between True and False Mask and True and False Creative Mind; his phase may not be the phase of his age, in which case he will have to make voluntary adjustments, and . . . the doctrine of the Thirteenth Cycle was to make the will even more free.'[5] All the same, Yeats was haunted by determinism—partly fascinated and partly repelled, as he was by the era of violence he foresaw for the world in the next cycle. As Ellmann observes, man's relation to the phases is variable, and this is enough to redeem the system from the determinist grip; but many people threatened by a fatalist system feel that if they can only introduce a joker into the pack their assurance of freedom will be strengthened. There are those happy souls who in a climate of scientific materialism convince themselves that Heisenberg's Uncertainty Principle is enough to bring back God, Freedom and Immortality. The Thirteenth Cone is Yeats's joker. *What* it is and where it fits into the system is impossible to say; but it is there as a charm or talisman to enhance the obscurer assertions of man's freedom.

Ellmann is persuaded that the Thirteenth Sphere or Cycle is Yeats's equivalent for God; but though the language used of it at the end of *A Vision* is exalted I do not think it reaches as far as that; Fate or Fortune perhaps, but not God. As he brings his argument to a close (VB 301-2) Yeats finds himself in possession of the algebraic formula that explains existence, and thinking of the future of his civilisation, he tries to substitute particulars for its abstractions. He ought by this means to know all things . . . but nothing comes. Then he realises that he has said all that can be said; the particulars are the work of the Thirteenth Cycle, and it will not reveal its secrets. That does not look like freedom; it looks rather as though we escape from one determinism to fall into another. But perhaps we are to understand, though it is never plainly stated, that the Thirteenth Cycle, 'which can do all things and knows all things', is an escape from the determined revolution of the gyres, not only into the realm of the unpredictable, but also into the realm of human volition and human choice; that superimposed on the machinery of the twelve cycles which nothing can alter or turn aside we find in the end a volition and a choice, and that the last word on human destiny is theirs.

22. But what ought to be the last word of *A Vision* never really gets uttered. Summing up his work in the first version of the book Yeats says 'I have not even dealt with the whole of my subject, perhaps not even with what is most important, writing nothing about the Beatific Vision, little of sexual love.' (VA xii) And the second version does nothing to repair these omissions. In most of the occultist creeds we find a complicated *process*, with an elaborate series of mediations, between earthly life and the celestial state, its ultimate goal. In Yeats's case the interest seems to be more in the process than in the goal. In Golden Dawn ethics a distinction is made between those who follow 'the path of the arrow', who aim directly at the mystic vision shunning all intermediate distractions, and those who, intending ultimately the same goal, follow the winding course of

experience, passing through all the phantasms offered by the intellect, the senses, and the imagination on the way. Yeats belongs to the second type. We are reminded of what his father said to him 'Your interest is in *mundane* things, whether beyond the stars or not.' The Beatitude is mentioned in both VA and VB only as a stage, briefly enjoyed, in the life of the soul between incarnations; and there is only the merest hint of its becoming, through the agency of the Thirteenth Cone, the ultimate bound and consummation of the whole process. What Yeats calls 'the condition of fire' is another name for the blessed state; but it too is recorded only as a transitory and occasional grace. (M 364–5, CP 281–3). And there is little sign anywhere in Yeats of the longing to escape from the wheel of rebirth that pervades Orphic and Indian thought.

Yeats valued his human pride, but he is untainted with spiritual presumption, and made no claim personally to have reached the loftier and more abstract rungs of the Platonic ladder where the senses and the passions have long been left behind. His aim was to redeem passion, not to transcend it, and a beatitude that had passed beyond the bounds of earthly love could not be his ideal goal. It is not an accident that in the lines just quoted Yeats speaks of the Beatific vision and sexual love in the same breath. There are many indications that he saw the two not as opposed but as ultimately destined to become one. His occult speculations were always deeply entangled with his emotional life. From what we know of the automatic scripts it is evident that a great mass of them was concerned with the spiritual-erotic relations of Yeats

119

and his circle—his wife, Maud Gonne, Iseult Gonne and others. But Yeats firmly obliterated all that aspect of the revelation from the published work. In the poetry he had always practised a similar reticence. When Coventry Patmore in *Sponsa Dei* made an unguarded association between divine and sexual love Gerard Manley Hopkins said to him 'That's telling secrets'; and without any prompting from Christian orthodoxy a natural dignity and *pudeur* led Yeats too to feel that such secrets were best reserved. Only the hermit Ribh, Patrick's antithetical opponent, rapt between two rival ecstasies, is allowed in his *Supernatural Songs* a few riddling glimpses of that inapprehensible consummation.

Notes

ABBREVIATIONS: WORKS BY YEATS

A   *Autobiographies*, 1955.
CP   *Collected Poems*, 1950.
E   *Explorations*, 1962.
E & I *Essays and Introductions*, 1961.
M   *Mythologies*, 1959.
VA   *A Vision* (1925). Critical edition by G.M. Harper and W.K. Hood, 1978.
VB   *A Vision* (1937). Reprinted 1962.

I. THE OCCULT TRADITION

1. Norman Cohn, *The Pursuit of the Millenium*, 1957; C.S. Lewis, *English Literature in the Sixteenth Century*, 1954, pp. 4–13; Edgar Wind, *Pagan Mysteries in the Renaissance*, 1958; D.P. Walker, *Spiritual and Demonic Magic from Ficino to Campanella*, 1958; Frances Yates, *Giordano Bruno and the Hermetic Tradition*, 1964; *The*

Rosicrucian Enlightenment, 1972; Gershom Scholem, *Major Trends in Jewish Mysticism*, 1955.

2. In *The Permanence of Yeats*, ed. J. Hall and M. Steinmann, 1950, p. 344. It is only fair to add that a few sentences farther on Auden gives Yeats full credit for neglecting these snobbish considerations.

3. H.P. Blavatsky, *The Key to Theosophy*, 1869, reprinted 1968, pp. 83–4.

4. See Yates, *Giordano Bruno*, pp. 22, 28–9.

5. See Wind, *Pagan Mysteries*, pp. 14–16.

6. W.R. Inge, *The Philosophy of Plotinus*, 1923, Vol. I, pp. xiv–v, 25–70.

II YEATS'S BELIEFS

1. Ellic Howe, *The Magicians of the Golden Dawn*, 1972; G.M. Harper, *Yeats's Golden Dawn*, 1974. The Golden Dawn rituals have been published, in spite of vows of secrecy, in several places, most accessibly by Israel Regardie, *The Golden Dawns an account of the teaching, rites and ceremonies of the G.D..*, River Falls, Wisconsin, 1970. A briefer and more readable account of the essential Golden Dawn tenets, though it comes from a rather later period and a later phase of the movement, is to be found in Dion Fortune, *The Mystical Qaballah*, 1935, many times reprinted.

2. Harper, *op.cit.*, p. 269.

3. In Harper, *op.cit.*, pp. 257–68.

Notes

III MAGIC AND POETRY

1. Blavatsky, *Key to Theosophy*, pp. 183–4.
2. C.G. Jung, *Memories, Dreams, Reflections*, 1963, p. 306.
3. *Diaries of Virginia Woolf*, Vol. III, 1980, p. 329.

IV A VISION: QUERIES AND REFLECTIONS

1. Harold Bloom, *Yeats*, 1970, p. 217.
2. Helen Vendler, *Yeats's Vision and the Later Plays*, 1963, p. 9.
3. Bloom, *op.cit.*, p. 213.
4. Bertrand Russell, *History of Western Philosophy*, 1946 edn., p. 55.
5. Richard Ellmann, *Yeats, the Man and the Masks*, 1949, p. 230.

Acknowledgements

Acknowledgements are made to Michael Yeats, A.P. Watt Ltd., Macmillan London Limited and Macmillan Publishing Company New York, for permission to reprint the poem 'The Lover Mourns for the Loss of Love' by W.B. Yeats and the first stanza of the poem 'Mohini Chatterjee' by W.B. Yeats.

Index

127

Index